Theodore W Hopkins

The Doctrine of Inspiration

An outline historical study

Theodore W Hopkins

The Doctrine of Inspiration
An outline historical study

ISBN/EAN: 9783337183400

Printed in Europe, USA, Canada, Australia, Japan

Cover: Foto ©ninafisch / pixelio.de

More available books at **www.hansebooks.com**

DOCTRINE OF INSPIRATION:

AN

OUTLINE HISTORICAL STUDY.

BY

THEODORE W. HOPKINS.

[NOT PUBLISHED.]

ROCHESTER, N. Y.
PRINTED FOR THE AUTHOR.
1891.

COPYRIGHT.
1881.
BY THEODORE W. HOPKINS.

CONTENTS.

	PAGE.
INTRODUCTION, ...	1
HEATHEN DOCTRINE OF INSPIRATION, ...	2–8
Vedic—Buddhistic—Zoroastrian—Chinese—Mohammedan—Classic Pagan—General Conclusions.	
JEWISH DOCTRINE OF INSPIRATION TO THE CLOSE OF THE FIRST CENTURY. A. D., ...	8–13
Palestinian Judaism—Alexandrian Judaism—Testimony of Jewish Writers.	
CHRISTIAN DOCTRINE OF INSPIRATION—ANTE-NICENE PERIOD, A. D. 100–325, ...	13–24
Terms—Unity of Inspiration in Old and New Testaments—Extra-Canonical Inspiration—Nature of Inspiration—Degrees of Inspiration—Verbal Inspiration—General Conclusions.	
POST-NICENE AND SUBSEQUENT HISTORY OF INSPIRATION TO THE CLOSE OF ANCIENT CHRISTIANITY, A. D. 325–750, . .	24–29
Causes of Diminished Importance Attached to this Doctrine—Nature of Inspiration—Degrees of Inspiration—Verbal Inspiration—General Conclusions.	
DOCTRINE OF INSPIRATION IN THE MIDDLE AGES, A. D. 750–1517,	29–37
Views of Individual Writers in Chronological Order—Scholastics—Mystics—Forerunners of Reformation—Jewish Doctrine—General Conclusions.	
DOCTRINE OF INSPIRATION DURING THE REFORMATION ERA, A. D. 1517–1600, ...	37–45
Views of Leading Reformers—Followers of Great Reformers—Remarks on Apparent Inconsistencies in Attitude of Reformers toward Scriptures.	
DOCTRINE OF INSPIRATION IN THE SEVENTEENTH CENTURY, .	45–60
Lutheran—Reformed—Roman Catholic—Arminian—Socinian—Mystic—Opinion in England.	
DOCTRINE OF INSPIRATION IN THE EIGHTEENTH CENTURY, .	61–73
Causes of Modification of Rigid Theories—Rationalistic Writers—More Evangelical—Swedenborg—Opinion in England.	
DOCTRINE OF INSPIRATION IN THE NINETEENTH CENTURY, .	73–106
German Rationalists—Schleiermacher—Supernaturalism—More General Evangelical—French Orthodoxy—Opinion in England—Greek and Roman Catholic Churches.	
GENERAL CONCLUSIONS FROM THE WHOLE SURVEY,	106–108
See Index of Authors ad. fin.	

The Doctrine of Inspiration:

An Outline Historical Study:

INTRODUCTION.

The accompanying sketch does not aim to present a complete critical history of the Doctrine of Inspiration. It simply embodies the results of some special studies, which may be of interest in view of current biblical and theological discussions.

It will be noticed that the method of treatment is not uniform. Somewhat frequent changes of plan were necessitated by the varying nature and amount of the material at command. In the latter part of the essay it has been deemed advisable to allow writers to speak, partially at least, for themselves, though great condensation has been necessary in order to bring detailed statements within a reasonable compass.

The author feels it due to himself to state that while he has endeavored to keep this sketch, as far as possible, free from subjective coloring, his personal convictions and sympathies are wholly in the direction of conservative orthodox opinions.

The science of Comparative Religion teaches that many ideas commonly associated with Christianity alone, and supposed to be its exclusive property, really belong to man as a religious being. No matter how rude the conception or imperfect their expression, they enter into every form of faith, and are coëxtensive with a belief in Deity. In other systems they voice deep needs of human souls and earnest though impotent efforts to supply them;

in Christianity the wants are fully met, the ideas become glorious realities.

Such an idea is that of Inspiration, in the broad sense of the word. In the historical survey proposed, we must be content to employ the term, as past ages have done, with some latitude of meaning, leaving nice distinctions and close definitions to the province of doctrinal polemics. We shall not undertake a study of the subject in its more general relations to the canon, but shall confine our investigations in the main to two specific points: the *Nature*, and the *Extent of Inspiration*.

A. THE HEATHEN DOCTRINE OF INSPIRATION.

I. The Vedic.

Nowhere in the world have such elaborate and minute theories of inspiration been developed as in western and southern Asia — especially in India. The Brahmans teach that even before time was, the Vedic hymns in their minutest parts lived in the mind of Deity, and were immediately communicated, not to common men, but to superior beings raised up and prepared to receive them. Of course but one element, the divine, is conceded in their composition; no room is left for trace or tinge of human coloring. With such an origin and character, they must form for the Hindu an absolutely infallible revelation.

Sanscrit scholars tell us that these high claims are nowhere put forth in the hymns themselves,[1] though the authors at times vaguely assert the presence of a higher consciousness and influence under which they wrote. Thus they would declare their felt dependence on an unseen Power, self-surrender to a higher Will — this and nothing more. But from such a small beginning there gradually grew up among the ancient Brahmans a belief in the supernatural origin and character of the Vedas, which was at last formulated into the extreme and artificial theory of inspiration above described. The same attribute is now ascribed also to the

---

[1] *Chips from a German Workshop*, I. 18.

Brahmanas (commentaries on the ancient Vedic sacrificial rites and the hymns therewith connected), but to no other Hindu writings.

II. The Buddhistic.

Buddhism can be properly understood only when viewed as a reaction against Brahmanism. Properly speaking, it is not a religion at all, for it has no real Deity; it is rather a metaphysical philosophy,—a system, not revealed, but discovered by a man, Gautama. Even after the sage attained the final truth, becoming Buddha, the Enlightened, he left in his gospel of annihilation no room for nature, much less for the supernatural.

Buddhism began by denying the authenticity and revealed character of the Vedas, but yet went on to develop an immense sacred canon of its own (two hundred and twenty-five folio volumes), for which, however, it dare make no claim of divine origin, or any sort of inspiration whatever. For our purposes, therefore, the system of Sakya-Mouni, though in *form* a book-religion, may be left out of the account.

III. The Zoroastrian.

Tradition among the Parsis ascribes the immediate and exclusive authorship of the whole Zend-Avesta to Ahura-Mazda, who delivered it complete to Zoroaster, that he might publish its contents among men.

The sacred books themselves, however, as now extant, make no such lofty assertions on their own behalf. The Yasna, not the Vendidad, according to Haug, does claim to be a divine revelation, but not in such a sense as to imply pure passivity on the part of the human organ. Zoroaster is admitted to immediate intercourse with the Deity, plies him with questions on every subject of great interest and moment, and receives full and trustworthy replies, which he makes known to his immediate followers and to mankind in general.

It is highly probable that Zoroaster committed none of his doctrines to writing. Like the Vedic hymns, they were transmitted through many centuries by oral tradition alone. The first penmen in each case are of necessity unknown.

It thus appears that the development of the doctrine of inspiration was substantially the same in the case of the Persian canon as in that of the Hindu.

IV. The Chinese.

It has been said of the three great religions of China, Confucianism, Buddhism and Taoism, that in their true conception they are not religions at all, as having no personal God; but that they are rather systems of philosophy, one moral, another metaphysical, and a third materialistic. If this be so, none of the sacred books can logically claim divine origin, or the attribute of inspiration in any form. The facts as established by modern scholarship seem to show:

1. That the idea of revelation, *as a possibility*, is common to both Confucianism and Taoism.

Dr. Legge says: "Among the primitive characters of the Chinese was one, symbol of manifestation or revelation from above. That God should make known his will from above, did not seem strange to the Chinese fathers. In 'Shih' we read: 'God spake to king Wan,' as in the Old Testament God spake to Moses. Hundreds of Taoist tracts are circulated in China purporting to be the teaching of this god or that, warning or advising mankind."[1]

2. As *matter of fact*, however, according to the same author, the various sacred books of China do not profess to have been inspired or to constitute what we should call a revelation. Historians, poets, or others wrote them as they were moved in their own minds. An old poem may occasionally contain what it says was spoken by God, but we can only understand that language as calling attention emphatically to the statement to which it is prefixed.[2]

V. The Mohammedan.

Though chronologically out of place, it is most convenient to notice here the view of inspiration implied in the Koran.

Mohammed professed to be the recipient of manifold visions and revelations, which came to him, not in waking, self-conscious

---

[1] *Religions of China*, p. 245.
[2] *Sacred Books of the East*, Vol. III., Introduction, xv.

moments, but in fits of ecstasy. The appearance of his person at such times was repulsive, terrible. "He roared like a camel; his eyes rolled and glowed like red coals, and on the coldest day terrible perspiration would break out all over his body. When the terror ceased, it seemed to him as if he had heard bells ringing, 'the sound whereof seemed to rend him to pieces,'—as if he had heard the voice of a man,—as if he had seen Gabriel,—or as if words had *been written in his heart*."[1] When the paroxysm was over and consciousness returned, then, and not before, did Mohammed begin to dictate to scribes that which he had heard in the state of ecstasy.

The prophet was a victim of epilepsy, but no diagnosis of this disease could explain all these symptoms with their attendant results. They seemed intelligible only as signs of the veritable prophetic frenzy. Thus classic paganism would have interpreted them, and it was quite natural that the religious credulity of the seventh century should do the same.

Turn now to the Koran. It purports to be a *direct revelation* from God in the highest sense. The inner consciousness of the prophet is not elevated and illumined with celestial light; rather is the human element driven from every nook and hiding place, while the divine element is sole and supreme. Every word individually, from the beginning to the end, is the direct utterance of Allah. "The formula, 'Speak, thus saith the Lord,' either precedes every single sentence, or must be so understood."

It is to be observed that this extreme and artificial theory of inspiration is not, as in the case of the Vedas and the Zend-Avesta, a gradual growth of ages, but rather an original claim made by Mohammed himself. When demand is now made for some miraculous sign of his prophetic mission and authority, Mussulmans appeal to the Koran itself as the most stupendous of all miracles. It is eternal and uncreated, being first written in the highest heavens, but carried by Gabriel to the lowest heaven, and thence at intervals made known to the prophet. As the immediate handiwork of God, it is faultless in style and inimitable in its beauty, but is for this very reason untranslatable into foreign tongues. The doctrine of inspiration could no farther go. It would be interesting, but is perhaps impossible to know,

---

[1] *Literary Remains of Immanuel Deutsch*, 81.

whether and how far its development in Mohammedanism was influenced by crude and exaggerated views prevalent in the corrupt Christianity and Judaism of the time and region.

VI. Classic Paganism.

It has been said, somewhat rashly perhaps, that "we search the literature of Greece and Rome in vain for the idea of *revelation*." If the affirmation be restricted to book-revelation, it may, perhaps, be approximately true, though the Sibylline books with their sacred character and supposed divine origin should count for something. But the idea of revelation in itself was common to the whole ancient world, and was nowhere more generally credited than in Greece and Rome. What else mean the Dodonian, Delphic and numerous other oracles, the Pythian priestess, the various sibyls, and the whole class of seers, soothsayers and diviners?

Apollo was the special god of prophecy, and he as well as other deities made known the future and all other needful matters of command and counsel through inspired human organs. Inspiration had its certain signs; its outward phenomena and internal characteristics were carefully analyzed and noted. Even the means of inducing it were discovered, so that to classic paganism it became an art.

There is no need of repeating the story of the distressing signs under which the Pythian priestess uttered her responses. The lofty tripod on which she sat, the smoke issuing from the well below, throwing her into delirium and convulsions, her wild and incoherent ejaculations, noted by attendants as the divine answer to anxious questionings,—all these are familiar to the intelligent schoolboy.

Pagan orthodoxy believed devoutly that Apollo himself dwelt in the priestess, prompting every word she spoke, annihilating for the time her human consciousness and personality, and making her his blind instrument. Even Plato could not rise above this vulgar idea, but maintained, with the Stoics and almost the whole of antiquity, that the sense for higher revelation arises in a condition of unconsciousness, in sleep, and most of all in ecstasy.

"No man, when in his senses, attains prophetic truth and inspiration; but when he receives the inspired word, either his intelligence is enthralled by sleep, or he is demented by some distemper or possession. And he who would understand what he remembers to have been said, whether he was in dream, or when he was awake, by the prophetic and enthusiastic nature, or what he has seen, must recover his senses."[1]

There were others, however, who took a different and a higher view. Plutarch, for example, excused the bad poetry with which sceptical ridicule charged the Pythian priestess, and yet maintained its inspiration by asserting that the deity made use of her imperfect natural faculties for conveying and embodying his own infallible truth. Here he clearly distinguishes two elements and factors in inspiration, a divine and a human, and seeks by attributing to each its proper share in the complex product, to avoid either extreme, credulity or unbelief.

He says: "We are not to believe that the god made the verses; but, after he has communicated the moving impulse, each of the prophetesses is moved in a way that corresponds to her own peculiar nature. For let us suppose that the oracles were not to be spoken, but recorded in writing, we should not, I imagine, ascribe to the god the strokes of the letters, and find fault with him because the writing was not so beautiful as that of the imperial edicts. Not the language, nor the tone, nor the expression, nor the measure of the verse comes from the god — all this comes from the woman. He simply communicates the intuitions, and kindles up a light in the soul with regard to the future."[2] More to the same purport might be quoted.

General Conclusions.

Enough has probably now been said respecting extra-Christian views of inspiration. We see that the idea exists in various forms and degrees, and shall find that it exerted, in its Platonic form, much influence upon Alexandrian Judaism, and thus mediately at least upon Christianity.

Two things at this stage of our inquiries demand notice.

1. It is not true, without exception, as commonly supposed, that heathen inspiration acknowledges but one factor, the divine,

---

[1] Plato, *Timæus*, 71, 72. Jowett's Trans., vol. II., 563.
[2] *De Pythiæ Oraculis*, cxxi.

and that it wholly suppresses — absolutely obliterates, for the time — the human consciousness of its organ. There are at least intimations of the conscious coëxistence and coöperation of the divine and human.

2. Extravagant, artificial, and rigidly mechanical theories of inspiration are not always the immediate and inevitable accompaniment of a sacred canon. As in the case of the Vedic hymns and the Zend-Avesta, they are apt to be the result of a long and gradual growth of tradition and superstition.

B. THE JEWISH DOCTRINE OF INSPIRATION, TO THE CLOSE OF THE FIRST CENTURY.

It may be said in general that the Jews always and all of them cherished a deep reverence for their sacred books, conceding their divine origin and their unique and binding authority. The specific doctrine or theory of inspiration, however, was a gradual growth, and was formulated mainly at Alexandria during the period between the cessation of prophecy and the close of the Old Testament canon. Opinions on this subject varied somewhat.

I. Palestinian Judaism.

It is here that we would naturally expect to find prevalent the strictest views on this subject. Two degrees of inspiration (not three as in the case of Maimonides and other Jewish doctors of the Middle Ages) were admitted.

1. *Legal or Mosaic.*

This was peculiar to Moses alone, being shared by no other one of the sacred writers. The Law came direct from God, being either written by his own hand, or else dictated to Moses as his amanuensis.[1] As to inherent character, it is in itself an original and perfectly sufficient revelation, and if Israel had acted in a worthy manner, no further divine communication through the other sacred books would have been needful.

Nothing is contained in the Hagiographa which is not implied

---

[1] Cremer in Herzog, *Real Encyclopädie*, art. *Inspiration.*

in the Law, nor dare any prophet give utterance to anything which is not founded on the same. All indeed which the prophets afterwards predicted was already beforehand revealed from Sinai.

The Law is called Holy Scripture *absolutely*, the other writings attain a like dignity only from their constituent relation to this.[1]

2. *Prophetic.*

All the other books of the Old Testament, though divinely revealed, must take a second rank.[2] This results from the fact that they reveal nothing new in substance, but simply teach the correct understanding and explanation of the Law. The difference of the two classes of writings was illustrated by the saying that 'Moses looked upon a clear mirror, other prophets upon one whose surface was dim'; or, that 'he looked through one, other prophets through several mirrors.'[3] Notwithstanding this lower degree of inspiration and consequent inferiority of rank, Palestinian Jewish theology insisted upon the inclusion of the Prophets and Hagiographa with the Law in 'Holy Scripture.' Those who denied the claim were branded as apostates from Israel.

It was not held that the process of inspiration in these writers annihilated their human personality and made them unconscious organs of the Spirit.[3] It did not even obliterate diversities of gifts, or peculiarities of literary style by which the productions of one might be distinguished from those of another. Apparently, more pronounced individuality was conceded to the writers of the historical books than to the prophets strictly so called.

II. Alexandrian Judaism.

Very different was the case with Alexandrian Judaism. Seemingly more liberal in general character, its theory of inspiration was far more strict. This is seen in the credit given to the fable of the miraculous origin of the Septuagint translation. Aristeas, followed by Philo and Josephus, relates that Ptolemy Philadelphus summoned seventy-two rabbins from Palestine to make a translation of the sacred books from the Hebrew original into

---

[1] Weber, *Alt-Synagogal. Palæstin. Theol.*, 78–80.

[2] Weber, *Alt-Synagogal. Palæst. Theol.*, 78.

[3] Cremer, 747.

Greek. These men performed the task, translating each one by himself, in a separate cell, in such a way that their productions agreed exactly, word for word, from beginning to end. Such unity could be attributed, as Irenæus says,[1] only to immediate divine inspiration.

This legend was generally credited, and greatly influenced the development of the doctrine of inspiration; in fact, it shows how lofty was the idea then already prevailing. Of course, arguing from the less to the greater, any reverence given to the translation would be intensified in the case of the Hebrew original.

The Hellenistic view of inspiration, if generally less elaborate and exact in form and statement than the Palestinian Jewish, was grosser, more extravagant, and mechanical in character. It assigned the rank of prophet to all Old Testament writers. All spoke and wrote in a state of ecstasy, which was normal to one under the influence of inspiration. Self-consciousness and free-will were suspended, and the seer became the merely passive organ of the Holy Ghost.

III. Testimony of Jewish Writers.

Of express testimonies to the inspiration of the Jewish canonical books, we can notice but three.

1. *The Apochryphal Writers.*

These bear clear and abundant witness to their belief in the divine origin and character of the Old Testament Scriptures. Moses is spoken of as 'commanded by God to write his Law;' the Law itself is 'the book of the covenant of the Most High God.'[2] Comfort is said to be derived from the 'holy books of Scripture, which we have in our hands.' The communications made to Moses and other sacred writers bear the character of divine revelations, and are the words of God himself.[3]

2. *Josephus.*

Josephus, born at Jerusalem, and a member of the sect of the

---

[1] *Adv. Hær.*, Lib. III.: 24.

[2] Quoted Lee on Inspiration, 62.

[3] Bannerman on Inspiration, 117.

Pharisees, ought to serve as a representative example of Palestinian Jewish orthodoxy. Indeed, he is quoted by most orthodox writers as a valuable witness to the general acceptance of the doctrine of plenary and verbal inspiration among his countrymen. He says: "Every one is not permitted, of his own accord, to be a writer, nor is there any disagreement in what is written ; they being only prophets that have written the original and earliest accounts of things, as they learned them of God himself, by inspiration ; and others have written what hath happened in their own time, and that in a very distinct manner also. For we have not an innumerable multitude of books among us, disagreeing from and contradicting one another, [as the Greeks have], but only twenty-two books, which contain the records of all past times, which are justly believed to be divine."[1] If this correctly represents the Jewish orthodoxy of the first century A. D., it does not necessarily indicate the personal opinions of the author. It seems doubtful whether Josephus had any real belief in the inspiration of the Old Testament Scriptures. If he had, how could he treat them as he does, while claiming to make them the basis of his own history? How could he jumble together fact and fancy, divine wisdom and foolish philosophy, veritable history and baseless tradition ? Why should he be so anxious to eliminate, by any and every possible method, the miraculous and Messianic elements from the narrative with which he has to deal ? It will probably be hard to find such an answer to these questions as will save the consistency and character of the author. Still, the testimony of Josephus, such as it is, is one which, in the meagreness of our information, we could ill afford to lose.

3. *Philo.*

This learned Alexandrian is generally, and on the whole correctly, taken as the representative of the Hellenistic Jewish view of inspiration. What has been said above of the general view (II.) will for the most part apply to him. When his opinions are subjected to a close examination, they are found to be vague, especially on the psychological phenomena in question—how much or how little activity he would assign to the personal

---

[1] *Contra Apion*, Lib. I.: cap. 7, 8.

mental powers of inspired men. He may have entertained mutually conflicting ideas on the whole subject.

When under the influence of inspiration, a person was in a state of ecstasy; and this to Philo was the 'goal of ambition,' and, as he testifies, in some sense a matter of personal experience with him. He claims inspiration not only for himself, but for every pious man; and yet he by no means attempts to place his own productions, or those of his fellows, on a level with Holy Scripture. His idea of ecstasy implies such a perfect self-surrender to the fellowship and influence of Deity, as to result in a complete suppression of the human consciousness and will before those which are divine. "The prophet," he says, "is the interpreter of the Deity, and God uses him as an instrument to make known what he will. A prophet says nothing of his own, but merely what another inspires within him."

Somewhat inconsistently with his magical view of inspiration, Philo admits a difference of *degree* in the same. In the *highest* (ἑρμηνεία) the utterances are immediately from God; the human element wholly recedes, the divine only comes to view, and that pure and unmixed. There is a union, or rather absorption of the person inspired in the God who moves and speaks within him. In the *second* or *intermediate* stage, there is a mingling of the purely divine with the human, both of which appear; the prophet questions and God replies (as in the Zend-Avesta); thus he is able to predict the future with infallible certainty. In the *lowest* stage, the inspiration proceeds from the divine, which has become the personal possession of the prophet. The latter speaks in his own name from his own consciousness, though the substance of the message is from God.

Careful scrutiny shows that at the bottom of Philo's idea of prophetic ecstasy there is no higher element than is drawn from heathen divination and mystery-worship. His syncretistic system allowed him to transfer the heathen conceptions of μαντική, or 'divine possessions,' to the prophets of the Old Testament. But more than this, the whole Philonic (and thus far, Hellenistic) theory is of heathen origin.

Conceding, as all critics do, the immense influence which Philo exerted ultimately upon this, as well as upon the whole circle of Christian doctrine, it is not enough to admit, with Hagenbach, that the external form of the theory of inspiration was *mixed up* with heathen notions; the pagan conception entered into and largely determined that of early Christianity. Valuable, then, as is Philo's witness, from the historical and apologetic points of view, his influence upon the actual development of the doctrine was to a great extent unwholesome and disastrous.

C. THE CHRISTIAN DOCTRINE OF INSPIRATION.—ANTE-NICENE PERIOD.

I. Terms.

The word θεοπνευστία (borrowed from 2 Tim. 3: 16,) was first made current in ecclesiastical language by Origen and Chrysostom. It became the most common term to express our modern English idea of inspiration. In the old Greek church, the meaning of the expression was indefinite. Most theologians, however, understood it, doubtless, in an active, rather than a passive sense—'full of the divine Spirit,' 'God-breathing' (Gott-athmend). The passive signification, 'breathed into,' 'in-spired by God,' appears to have been made prominent by Chrysostom; later it become controlling in the church.

The Latin word *inspiration*, first applied by Tertullian to the sacred books, and thus introduced into the dogmatic Christian vocabulary, occurs in many passages of the Vulgate, where a divine 'breathing,' 'breathing upon,' is mentioned, but it answers not so much to the word θεοπνευστία, as to the ἐπίπνοια of the old Greeks,—a word which in the Christian church also came to possess precisely the same signification as θεοπνευστία.[1]

II. Unity of Inspiration in the Old and New Testaments.

With the Jewish canon, passed over also to the primitive Christians, naturally and inevitably, Jewish ideas and views of *its* inspiration. From the very first, the apostolic writings were regarded with great reverence, and were considered as authoritative for those to whom they were immediately addressed. No complete

---

[1] Münscher, *Lehrb. Dogm.-gesch.* (Neudecker), II: 2, 220.

collection of Christian sacred writings, however, had yet been made; and consequently the precise relation of those already known and used, to the Old Testament Scriptures was not definitely settled in the consciousness of the Church. Certainly the formulated theory of Jewish inspiration was not at the outset applied to them. This application, however, was speedily made, and several things conspired to effect it. One was the habit of reading sections from the writings of the prophets and apostles in the public assemblies of the Christians.[1] Equal dignity seemed thus to be ascribed to both. Then, again, careful scrutiny disclosed the indissoluble internal connection and unity of both: the one, as containing the predictions of the Messiah and his mission of salvation; the other, as proclaiming his actual advent, and the completion of his redeeming work.

Witness as to the belief of the church in the common divine origin and character of both classes of sacred books is abundant, clear and decisive.

Thus Justin († 163) says: "We have believed God's voice, spoken again by the apostles of Christ, and proclaimed by the prophets."[2]

Theophilus: "Concerning the righteousness which the Law enjoined, confirmatory utterances are found, both within the Prophets and in the Gospels, because they all spoke inspired by one Spirit of God."[3]

Yet more distinctly, Irenæus († 202): "For the one and same Spirit of God, who proclaimed by the prophets what and of what sort the advent of the Lord should be, announced also that the fulness of the times had come."[4]

Of Tertullian († cir. 230), an old German writer says: "His whole theory is summed up in these two propositions: 'The Old and New Testaments are inspired; and, both collections of writings are inspired by one and the same God.' This he proves in detail, in his treatise 'Against Marcion,' especially Chapters xix., xxv.

---

[1] Justin Martyr, *First Apol.*, c. lxvii.

[2] *Dial. cum Tryph.*, c. cxix.

[3] *Ad Autol.*, III : 12.

[4] *Adv. Hær.*, iii : 21, 4.

Origen's testimony is peculiarly clear and explicit. In the preface to his treatise *De Principiis*, (c. 4), he says: "That this Spirit inspired each one of the saints, whether prophets or apostles, and that there was not one Spirit in the men of the old dispensation, and another in those who were inspired at the advent of Christ, is most clearly taught throughout the churches."

Cyril of Jerusalem, living at the end of our period, maintained that the same Spirit spoke through prophets and apostles: "Let no man divide the Old from the New Testament, or say that the Spirit in one is different from the Spirit in the other, else he offends against the Holy Ghost himself."[1]

Much more testimony to the same effect, both direct and indirect, might be drawn from the ante-Nicene writers, but it seems unnecessary.

Thus not only did the ante-Nicene church acknowledge the unity and equality of the inspiration of the Old and New Testaments, but various circumstances conspired to increase the emphasis placed upon it. Chief among these was the opposition of the Gnostics, who either wholly rejected the Old Testament, maintaining that it was inspired by the Demiurge; or, as Irenæus says of the Valentinians, ascribed great difference in character, not only to the prophetic books, but even to the discourses of Christ, according as they were inspired by higher or lower, more or less perfect spiritual principles.

III. Extra-Canonical Inspiration.

Destructive critics have made much of the fact that the idea of inspiration was not strictly limited by the early church-fathers to the canonical writings, but was extended by some to the apochryphal books of the Old Testament, and to post-apostolic Christian writings. We see, for example, that—

Justin Martyr and Theophilus attributed inspiration to the Sibylline books, and those of the Persian Hystaspes. Clement of Alexandria († cir. 220) appears to hold that every extraordinary talent and all knowledge of the true and good is the result of divine influence—is inspired. He also says that among heathen

---

[1] *Catechesis*, XVI : 4.

as well as Jews, God endowed distinguished men with prophetic gifts. He here refers to philosophers.

Tertullian gives the impression that he also regarded every writing useful for edification as inspired.[1]

Origen († 254), thought that perhaps a place in the canon should be assigned to the Shepherd of Hermas.

Cyprian († 258) declared that he was favored with visions, and speaks of writing certain epistles under the inspiration of God.[2]

These facts do indeed show that the ideas of these church-fathers upon the subject of inspiration were in some respects indefinite, but the reason is not far to seek. Some of them were acquainted with the Old Testament only as existing in the version of the Seventy, and therefore were inclined to view it with that reverence which later orthodoxy accorded only to the Hebrew original. It is to be remembered also that the canon of the New Testament was not yet finally determined in the consciousness of the church. More accurate investigations in this department had yet to be made. A more exact definition of inspiration itself had yet to be supplied, and a more scientific theory of the same to be developed.

On the other hand, it is to be observed that the church never committed itself to the sanction of any of the doctrinal vagaries of individual fathers with reference to the sacred Scriptures and their divine inspiration. Certain it is that 'always, everywhere and by all' a higher *degree* of inspiration was attributed to the Old and New Testaments than to any other writings, one that implied a clear and absolute infallibility of essential contents, and a unique divine character.

Clement of Alexandria, who perhaps dwells more at length than any other ante-Nicene writer upon this aspect of the subject, while he concedes a kind of inspiration to the philosophers, and thinks the Holy Ghost had imparted some truths to them, in other passages expressly concedes that they have fallen into error; but he says of the Old and New Testaments: "I could cite many other passages of which no point remains unfulfilled, for the mouth of the Lord, the Holy Ghost, has spoken it."[3]

---

[1] *De Cultu Fem.*, c. 3.

[2] *Epist.* lxiii., lxxvii.

[3] *Cohort. ad Gentes*, c. 9.

Tertullian declared that the apostles were made possessors of the *fulness* of the Holy Ghost, while all others shared his gifts only *in measure*.[1] This would probably express the general judgment of the ancient church concerning his divine relation to the different classes of writings.[2]

IV. The Nature of Inspiration.

No formal definition of inspiration, nor any connected systematic doctrine of the same was established during the period with which we are now concerned.

At the very first, the church seems to have contented herself with the conviction of the apostolic authority of the authors, and the conceded truth of the contents of the sacred books. Soon, however, questionings began to arise respecting the *nature* of the divine influence under which the various writers did their work. Two diverging views were developed among the ante-Nicene fathers.

1. The first and stricter one was, as is evident, of heathen origin, and was mixed up with ideas of heathen soothsaying. Starting from the idea of the *prophet* as the interpreter of Deity, —a conception common to Christianity with other forms of faith— it taught an overwhelming of the human mind and spirit by divine power, though probably never in such an absolute and unqualified sense as in Montanism and classic paganism.

2. The second more sober and liberal theory had its source in Palestinian Judaism, and conceives the divine influence as exerted rather in the way of 'in-spiriting,' furthering and assisting the life and the writing of the holy men.

The real difference between the two views was involved in the question at issue, viz.: Whether the condition of ecstasy in

---

[1] *Exhort. ad Cast.*, c. 4.

[2] If *some* of the ante-Nicene fathers did fail to grasp (and this is by no means certain) the generic and fundamental distinction between supernatural inspiration bestowed upon prophets and apostles, and mere divine illumination vouchsafed to them and their contemporaries, they were only the precursors of a long array of reputedly able and orthodox writers on inspiration in the church of the eighteenth and nineteenth centuries, whose ideas upon this point are certainly confused.

the penmen was essential as a guarantee of the supernatural character of the prophecies and other Scriptures.

Representatives of the former opinion were found chiefly among the Apologists.

Justin Martyr speaks of the divine plectrum itself descending from heaven, and using righteous men like a harp or lyre.[1]

Again: "When you hear the utterances of the apostles, spoken as it were personally, you must not suppose that they are spoken by the inspired themselves, but by the divine Word who moves them."[2]

Athenagoras employs a figure similar to that of Justin, saying: "The Spirit made use of the prophets, as a flute-player breathes into a flute."[3]

He also describes the condition of those who were under the influence of inspiration, as a condition of ecstasy. "Moses, Isaiah, Jeremiah and other prophets, lifted in ecstasy above the natural operations of their own minds, by the impulses of the divine Spirit, uttered the things with which they were inspired."[4]

Theophilus similarly calls the sacred writers 'instruments, organs of God.'

The use of the figure of musical instruments in this connection was probably borrowed from Philo, and shows that as his mind was impregnated with heathen notions concerning the nature and process of inspiration, so the minds of most of the Apologists were tainted with the same. This indeed seems natural, when we remember that they were trained in heathenism, and that their first knowledge of Christian truth was not the result of logical thought, but was referred solely to revelation and the action of the Spirit of God. The whole conception could not fail to receive powerful impression from traditional habits of thought respecting the Sibyls, the Pythian priestess and other seers and soothsayers of antiquity. The evidence here is cumulative, and cannot be given in detail, but will repay careful study,[5] provided only it be constantly borne in mind that the idea of

---

[1] *Cohort. ad Græc.*, c. viii.

[2] *First Apol.*, c. xxxvi.

[3] *Legat. pro Christ.*, c. ix.

[4] *Ad Autol.*, ii. 9.

[5] Nitzsch, *Dogm.-gesch.*, 259–60.

prophecy formed the point of departure in all discussions of this age upon the nature of the inspiration of the sacred books.[1]

[It is worthy of note, in passing, that Rudelbach, in common with various other orthodox writers, has made labored, though ineffectual attempts,[2] to clear Justin Martyr and other early fathers from the charge of holding essentially heathen ideas upon the nature of inspiration. He seeks to explain away the inferences naturally drawn from their use of the figure of musical instruments, and thinks they did not with Philo make ecstasy a fundamental element of prophecy, nor teach a motionless and unconscious passivity, but rather an elevated and illuminated rational consciousness in the inspired seer. The apologetic and polemic aim, however, in Rudelbach, Lee[3], Bannerman,[4] and others who have attempted partial sketches of the development of the doctrine of inspiration, is stronger than the true historic instinct.]

The view thus indicated of prophetic inspiration, as presupposing a passive state of absolute receptivity, continued in the main the controlling one, until toward the middle of the third century. It reached its climax and wrought its own ruin in the fanatical excesses of Montanism, when God-sent madness or insanity was demanded as the test of the true prophet. The *subject* of inspiration here sank into a state of delirium and took leave of his senses; his spirit slept under the sole and forceful waking, moving influence of the Paraclete. Thus Tertullian says: "To grace ecstasy or rapture is incident. For when a man is rapt in the Spirit, especially when he beholds the glory of God, or when God speaks through him, he necessarily loses his sensation (*excidat sensu*), because he is overshadowed with the power of God."[5] Nitzsch thus comments: "The Montanists sought in ecstasy as a supernatural medium of the conception of the divine, at the same time the satisfaction of a kind of mystical voluptuousness; and, moreover, this is to them, not only

---

[1] Cremer, 747.
[2] *Zeitschr. für die Gesammt. Luth. Theol., Erst. Quart.*, 27.
[3] *Inspiration of the Scriptures*, 86–8.
[4] *Inspiration of the Scriptures*, 122–4.
[5] *Adv. Marc.*, iv : 22.

for the sacred writers, but above all for their own new prophets, the sufficient means of inspiration."[1]

From the time of Aurelius at least (A.D. 161-80), the more liberal view of inspiration had its advocates (though in a minority), and it indicated the progressive drift of thought; but only in the general reaction of the church against Montanism did it come to the surface, assert itself with energy, and finally after the middle of the third century become controlling in the church. The aim henceforward was the rigid exclusion of all heathen elements from the conception, especially the idea of ecstasy or suspension of the human consciousness in the sacred writers. A human as well as a divine side was reckoned to inspiration, the elevated self-consciousness and spontaneous activity of the person filled with the Holy Ghost. This freer view was chiefly, though not exclusively, represented in the school of Alexandria.

The author of the Clementine Homilies holds that the prophecy of the true prophet is not ecstatic; he does not speak in a state of madness, but knows what he says. Beholding it, he reveals it. And what he reveals, he reveals clearly, unambiguously. He does not utter doubts and uncertainties.

Miltiades, an Apologist, wrote, according to Eusebius,[2] a treatise in the reign of Aurelius, to prove that it was not needful for the prophet to speak in ecstasy.

Clement of Alexandria, in his *Stromata*, designates ecstasy as a characteristic of false prophets and of the Evil Spirit. If he compares mankind in general to an instrument upon which the Logos plays, it is in a very different sense from Philo and Athenagoras, who represent it as a merely passive organ of revelation.[3]

Origen, if not the pioneer in this process of theological purgation, certainly did much to establish upon grounds of reason, and to fix indelibly in the consciousness of the church the higher view which in his day was surely, if slowly and irregularly, working its way to recognition. He reckoned inspiration as belonging to the circle of church doctrines; and in the fourth book of his dogmatic work *De Principiis* devotes a special chapter

---

[1] *Dogm.-gesch.*, 261.

[2] *Hist. Eccles.*, v : 17.

[3] Nitzsch, *Dogm.-gesch.*, 262.

to it. He avoids the sensuous comparisons employed by the Apologists, and thus escapes their errors.

Origen made at least a first approach to a more exact definition of the nature and process of inspiration, understanding by it not the mere inpouring of foreign thoughts, but an elevation of the natural powers of the soul through the touch of the Holy Ghost.

Though he expresses doubts upon some important points, e. g., whether inspiration extends to every passage of the word of God, yet his heart and the general tenor of his teaching was true at bottom, as when he says in one of his homilies: "The holy books contain the fulness of the Spirit, and neither in the law, nor in the prophets, nor in the apostolic writings is there anything which has not its origin in the fulness of the divine Majesty."

The same general view was maintained by his pupils and successors.

V. Degrees of Inspiration.

We have seen above that both Palestinian and Alexandrian Judaism distinguish degrees in inspiration. The same thing is done by some of the ante-Nicene fathers, though from a different point of view.

Origen makes the degree of inspiration dependent upon the moral state of the subject, i. e., upon the measure of his moral and personal appropriation of the divine. He places the prophetic writings above all others, as beginning with 'Thus saith the Lord.' He values the gospels more highly than the epistles, because, though Jesus and Paul were both filled with the Holy Ghost, the vessel of the latter was much smaller than that of the former.[1] He speaks of the apostolic writings as 'full of wisdom and trustworthy,' but doubts whether Paul intended to range his own under the head of 'Scripture given by inspiration of God,' (2 Tim. 3 : 16). He calls attention to the fact that Paul makes a difference in the Second Epistle to the Corinthians, between what he said *in his own spirit*, and *in the spirit of Christ*. The former utterances, he says, 'are spoken under divine impulse, and have authority and weight, but are not to be

---

[1] *Homily on Luke*, xxix.

derived strictly and immediately from divine revelation."[1] [This is one of the points on which, as above indicated, there seems to have been some wavering in Origen's own mind.] He also ranks Paul one degree higher than Timothy and Luke, and finds greater perfection in Romans than in any other of the Pauline epistles.

2. Tertullian indeed admits degrees in inspiration, but refers them, not to the sacred writers as compared among themselves, but to Christ, the apostles and prophets on the one hand, and ordinary Christians on the other. His views, therefore, are not pertinent to our present inquiry.

3. Novatian taught[2] that the same Holy Spirit was in prophets and apostles, but to the former it was given only at certain times and in 'smaller measure, while upon the latter it was bestowed in its fulness, and as a perpetual endowment. This writer clearly held that the inspiration apparent in the *writings* of the apostles was not the result of a *special* divine influence, but was only a part of the general divine assistance vouchsafed them in all their work.

VI. Verbal Inspiration.

Did the early fathers extend the inspiration of the Holy Scriptures to their *form* and *expression*, as well as their substance? This is a most important question in connection with the ante-Nicene doctrine of inspiration. It is generally, though not universally, answered by writers on doctrine-history *in the affirmative*. The facts are substantially as follows:

Justin Martyr says: "The holy men needed no art of words nor skill in captious and contentions speaking," etc.[3]

Irenaeus seems not only to have believed in verbal inspiration in general, but (if we may deduce his general view from one special passage), to have held that the Holy Spirit selected the words from special foresight of the needs of future ages. Thus he remarks: "Matthew might certainly have said (in the beginning of his gospel), 'Now the birth of JESUS was on this wise;' but the Holy Ghost, foreseeing that corrupters would arise, (viz.,

---

[1] *Com. on Jno.*, Vol. I : c. 4.
[2] *De Trinitate*, c. 29.
[3] *Cohort. ad Graecos*, c. 8.

the Gnostics who wished to distinguish between Jesus and Christ) and guarding by anticipation against their deceit, says: 'But the birth of CHRIST was on this wise.'"[1]

Yet the same father acknowledges imperfections[2] in the style of Paul, and attributes them to the impetuosity and fire of the apostle—in short, to his temperament.

3. Tertullian seems clear and explicit in his declarations: "Our sacred Scriptures," he says, "are the very words and letters of God." As a Montanist he could consistently hold no other view than that of absolute dictation; yet expressions occur which it is hard logically to reconcile with this belief. His general position, however, cannot be considered doubtful.

4. Clement of Alexandria says: "Truly holy are those letters that sanctify and deify, and the writings that consist of those holy letters and syllables, this same apostle (Paul) calls inspired of God."[3]

5. Origen appears to accept verbal inspiration without qualification, holding that every iota of the Scriptures has a special value;[4] yet one finds scattered in his writings passages which seem inconsistent with this view, as e. g. when he calls attention to solecisms in the language of the sacred writers.

6. Eusebius[5] may be credited with the same opinion, since he considers 'each one who proposes to alter the words of the Bible as esteeming himself wiser than the Holy Ghost.'

From these and similar testimonies the inference may be drawn that among the ante-Nicene fathers verbal inspiration was in some sense a general article of faith, though some wavered, and it is hard to say just how much weight is to be given to individual utterances.

Nitzsch[6] endeavors to explain away the force of such testimonies as we have quoted above, and maintains that, apart from the ecstatics (Athenagoras, the Montanists, etc.,) no church teacher positively and consistently taught the theory of verbal inspiration.

---

[1] *Adv. Her.*, iii : 16, 2.

[2] Id., iii : 7, 2.

[3] *Cohort. ad Gentes*, c. ix.

[4] *Homily on Jeremiah.*

[5] *Hist. Eccl.*, v : 28.

[6] *Dogm.-gesch.*, 263.

General Conclusions.

As the general result of our survey of the history of the doctrine of inspiration during the first three centuries, we see that the Christian church inherited the idea as a legacy from the Jewish, and extended it to the writings of the New Testament. It was for the most part an article of faith, rather than the subject of curious speculations. No definite and artificial theory was as yet established. As a consequence, differing views as to the nature and extent of the same, and all doubtful utterances are to be referred, not to the great fact itself, but to the lack of clear and systematic doctrinal development.

D. POST-NICENE AND SUBSEQUENT HISTORY OF INSPIRATION TO THE CLOSE OF ANCIENT CHRISTIANITY. 325—750 A. D.

It will be convenient, for the sake of brevity, to group together the next four hundred and twenty-five years in one survey.

Henceforward inspiration and kindred questions occupy relatively a less important place in the development of doctrine. It is easy to account for this.

1. The age of apologies was past, and the Montanistic heresy had received its death-blow, so that there seemed neither reason nor interest in prolonging a war of words.

2. In the great doctrinal controversies which now emerged, and which for centuries engrossed the attention of the church, the subject did not come under special discussion. The *fact* of inspiration was universally conceded, as it always had been. The idea lay deep in the consciousness of the church, though the dogmatic conception was not as yet strictly and accurately defined.

3. A rival to the sole supremacy of the Scriptures was rapidly growing up within the church: viz., the authority of the hierarchy, especially that of the united body in council assembled. Conciliar decisions were viewed as inspired, therefore as infallible, and of binding force upon the conscience. They were proclaimed as utterances of Christ, or of the Holy Ghost. Inspiration thus came to be a permanent attribute of the body eccle-

siastical, and was no longer viewed as the exclusive possession of a written code.

I. The Nature of Inspiration.

In general throughout this long period, though perhaps more especially at its beginning and its close, ideas on this subject were strict—frequently exaggerated, sometimes utterly inconsistent. We notice—

1. That the theologians of the Nicene age inherited from their predecessors a tendency to emphasize strongly the difference between the inspiration of heathenism and that of their own sacred books. Eusebius attempted to set forth and explain the points of difference. A summary of his statements is given from an old German writer.

a. The oracular responses are absurd, immoral and impious, both in themselves and in the practical results to which they lead in human life. On the other hand, men who 'speak as moved by the Holy Ghost,' dissuade from idolatry and heathen crimes, and reveal Christ, the great Teacher and Redeemer.

b. Demoniac influence darkens the mind, and deprives it of the use of reason, so that the inspired appear frantic. The divine Spirit, on the other hand, who is himself the purest light, illumines the soul, and thus fits it for the apprehension of supersensuous things. The inspired remain sober and awake, understand and pass judgment on the things they utter.

c. Heathen oracles are made known through unworthy men or through animals; God's Spirit, on the other hand, honors only such men with his influence as have rendered themselves fit for the same by the practice of virtue.

2. It is clear, without further illustration, that the church held rigidly for a considerable period to the idea, so emphasized by Origen and others, of the *elevation* and *illumination*, not the *suppression* of the human consciousness of the person under divine influence.

3. Quite inconsistently, there was still a strong tendency among most of the Nicene and later fathers to make the sacred writers the mere instruments of the Holy Spirit, who is the sole author of Scripture, even in the process of recording.

[This is seen in the legend of the loss of the Jewish sacred writings during the Exile, and their restoration by Ezra through the power of the Holy Ghost.]

a. Chrysostom († 407) says that 'John and Paul in their writings did not speak themselves, but that God spoke through them.'[1]

He also calls the 'the mouth of the prophets and apostles the mouth of God.'[2]

b. Augustine († 430) speaks of the apostles as 'the hands who wrote down what was dictated by Christ the head.'[3] He calls Holy Scripture, 'the venerable stylus of the Holy Ghost,' and declares that 'no word and no syllable in the Bible is superfluous, and without great and deep meaning.'

"I have learned to render to those books of Scripture alone which are now called canonical, reverence and honor to such a degree that I most firmly believe that no one of the authors erred in writing anything."[4]

c. Theodoret († 457) held it to be a matter of indifference who wrote any of the sacred books, since the Holy Ghost was the *real* author.

d. Cassiodorus († 562) speaks of the Bible as ' a writing which was not invented by human reason, but by a heavenly power was poured into the holy men.' Here is represented the infusion both of ideas and words.

e. Gregory the Great († 604) said 'it was superfluous to ascertain the author of any book of the Bible, since the Holy Ghost was the real author of the same ;' and ' it was absurd when one read the writing of a great monarch to ask what pen it was written with.'

4. Though the activity of the Holy Ghost in inspiration was the main and generally engrossing thought, it is yet true that the human element was not wholly overlooked. Something was yet attributed to the individuality and spontaneity of the sacred writers themselves.

a. Chrysostom notices the alleged discrepancies in the Gospels, but attributes them to the nature and peculiarity of historical

---

[1] *Evangel. Joh.*, Hom. I.

[2] *Acta Apost.*, Hom. XIX.

[3] *De Consens. Evangel.*, I : 35.

[4] *Epist.* 82, I : 3.

composition as a human art.¹ Viewing them as intrinsically unimportant, he yet finds in them valuable evidence of the trustworthiness of the writers in all essential facts.²

c. Jerome († 420) entertained similar ideas. He had no hesitation in acknowledging peculiarities of expression and conception, and differences in less weighty matters among the apostles. These are of purely human, not of divine origin. He finds various literary defects in Paul's epistles, and more than these, some traces of a spirit not altogether Christian. Yet he views the whole human side of the Scriptures as subserving in God's providential order important apologetic ends.

c. Augustine, speaking of the minor differences of the Evangelists, says: " It is evident that they have set forth these matters just in accordance with the recollection which each retained of them, and just according as their several predilections led them to employ greater brevity or richer detail."³

d. Quite in the same line do Theodore of Mopsuestia († 429) and Theodoret, among the Antiochian church-teachers, affirm characteristic peculiarities in the human authors of Scripture, and in their methods of conceiving truth.

e. Basil the Great († 379) compares the sacred writers to mirrors, whose surfaces, according to the degree of their polish and clearness, condition the reception and reflection of the images.

5. From what has been already said, especially from the extracts given, one may form a general idea of patristic views as to the nature of inspiration in the fourth, fifth, and following centuries. From these views there were, in the case of individuals, notable deviations.

a. Theodore of Mopsuestia looked at the inspiration of the sacred books chiefly from the *human* point of view. He maintained, in regard to the writings of Solomon, i. e., Proverbs, Ecclesiastes and Canticles, that their author had not the gift of *prophecy*, but only that of *wisdom*. The Song of Songs was a merely human writing —an offensive poem of Solomon's, composed on the occasion of his illegal marriage with an Egyptian princess. Theodore dealt very

---

¹ Neander, *Hist. of Chr. Dogm.*, 1 : 280–1.
² *Homily on Matt.*, I : 2.
³ *De Consens. Evangel.*, II : 12 (p. 232).

freely also with the book of Job, censuring the author for ambition, and for offensive allusions to heathen mythology. Some truer ideas seem also to have taken possession of his mind. He made a distinction between the conscious thought and intent of the sacred writers themselves, and of the higher mind and meaning of the Spirit who spoke through them. He also combatted the ideas of those who were supremely bent on finding a full-fledged system of theology in the Old Testament. Unfortunately his zeal carried him too far in the opposite direction. For these and other heresies he was condemned by the Fifth Œcumenical Council, 553 A. D.

Equally unorthodox ideas appear in the writings of Junilius, an African bishop of the sixth century. Thus in answer to the question, 'How is the authority of the sacred books to be considered?' he replies: "Some are of perfect authority, some of partial authority, and some of none at all."[1] In the second class, he enumerates Job, Chronicles, Ezra, etc.; in the third, our Old Testament Apocrypha.

II. Degrees of Inspiration.

In regard to this it is sufficient to say that such difference was not and could not generally be admitted by the church of this age, being precluded by prevailing views as to the nature of the divine influence exerted upon the human organs. Certain writers, however, appear to favor it, viz.: Basil and Theodore of Mopsuestia just quoted.

III. Verbal Inspiration.

This was most commonly recognized, as will appear by consulting the citations given above under I : 1. It was believed that in the sacred records there exists nothing in any wise superfluous. Every word and syllable has an important aim, and every proposition embraces in itself an inexhaustible richness of thought.

IV. General Conclusions.

In one word, at the close of ancient Christianity, little interest was felt in the question of inspiration. It was quite overshad-

---

[1] *De Part. Div. Leg.*, I : 8.

owed by others of greater apparent importance. The strictest ideas prevailed both as to its nature and extent, but these were based upon merely mechanical assent to the statements of earlier fathers, and not upon any intelligent and impartial investigations of the facts and teachings of the sacred records themselves. There was a relapse toward the ideas and views of paganism and Alexandrian Judaism upon the subject. Like many other vital doctrines of theology, that of inspiration seemed to suffer a well-nigh total eclipse.

E. THE DOCTRINE OF INSPIRATION DURING THE MIDDLE AGES. 750—1517 A. D.

The Middle Ages constitute almost a blank in the history of the doctrine of inspiration—in fact quite a blank, so far as progressive development is concerned. The subject was indeed discussed in the general connection of the Scholastic system, but there was little interest in it, primarily because a continuously inspired church and infallible tradition occupied in the minds of the multitude the place of religious authority otherwise ascribed to an inspired book. The orthodox belief generally remained in the ascendant, but ideas were exaggerated and indefinite. This appears from the fact that now, as at the very first among the Apologists, *prophecy* formed the great centre around which the whole conception turned.

The utterances of the Mediæval theologians on inspiration are so few, vague and disjointed as to be incapable of classification under proper headings. We must be content here to state the views of a few authors in chronological order.

I. John of Damascus.

John of Damascus, († circ. 760), is the first writer who comes under our notice. Though he attempted the construction of a doctrinal system, and 'concentrated in himself the expiring energies of Greek theology,' yet he makes no definite deliverance on this subject. He employs revelation and Holy Scripture as interchangeable terms and says:[1] " By the Holy Ghost,

---
[1] *De Fide Orthod.*, IV., c. 17.

both law and prophets, evangelists, apostles, pastors and teachers spoke. 'All Scripture, therefore, is given by inspiration of God,' 2. Tim. 3: 16." Little more than this can be gleaned from his writings.

II. Fridegisus.

Fridegisus, Abbot of Tours and pupil of Alcuin, appears as an advocate of verbal inspiration in the most rigid sense, maintaining that the divine Spirit inspired not only the meaning of the Scriptures, their contents and methods of expression, but actually formed the very words in the mouths of the writers. He appears also to extend infallibility even to translators and commentators.[1]

III. Agobard.

Agobard, Archbishop of Lyons († 841) stoutly opposed these extreme views, and held them up to ridicule, by showing the absurd consequences to which they led.[2] He had some conceptions of, though he did not fully develop, the distinction of the divine and human elements in the Scriptures.[3] He conceded also the existence of grammatical inaccuracies there, which, however, should be attributed not to the Holy Ghost, but to man, who is responsible for the form of the language. The essence of inspiration consists in the general character of the contents, not in the mere words themselves.

IV. Euthymius Zigabenus.

Euthymius Zigabenus (about 1116) indirectly discloses his views respecting inspiration, when he accounts for the insertion of given particulars in one gospel, and their omission in another, by the fact of the greater or less completeness and exactness of the recollections of the writers. This again is explained by the fact that they composed their narratives at some considerable time after the occurrence of the events themselves.[4]

---

[1] Hagenbach, *Hist. Doct.*, 1: 425.

[2] *Adv. Fridegis.*, c. 12.

[3] Neander, *Church History*.

[4] *Comment. Matt.*, XII: 8.

V. Anselm.

Anselm, Archbishop of Canterbury († 1109) indulged in no sceptical questionings of the orthodox theory of inspiration, but set himself to give a rational account of the contents of his faith concerning it. He devoted whole nights to the consideration of various intricate questions connected with the dogma, especially how the prophets could view the future as present. By a broad generalization from a kind of vision in which he was enabled to look through a stone wall and see the monks celebrating mass, he concluded that as space had been annihilated for him, so the other dimension was done away for the prophets under inspiration. Things to come were revealed to them as present.

This method of argumentation certainly possessed the method of *originality*, if no other excellence.

VI. Abelard.

Abelard's († 1142) whole conception of the doctrine of inspiration was very loose. In the introduction to his *Sic et Non*, he explicitly denied that prophets and apostles were infallible.[1] He distinguished degrees in the bestowment of the divine influence, and held that the prophets did not always speak under the impulse of the Spirit, even when they thought they did. They were allowed to mingle truth with error, and the natural with the supernatural, in order to keep them humble, and lead them to discriminate more carefully between their own utterances and those proceeding from the Spirit of God.

VII. Thomas Aquinas.

Thomas († 1274) expresses himself upon the question of inspiration with more fulness, precision and clearness than is usual with the Scholastics. He makes God the author of Scripture, but like Abelard admits degrees in the divine influence exerted upon the sacred writers. He distinguishes express revelation from an instinct which the human mind may possess sometimes unconsciously. This *divine instinct* is a lower degree of inspiration than *prophetic certainty*.[2] Thomas also

---

[1] *Sic et Non.*, Edn. Cousin, p. 11.
[2] Baur, *Dogm.-gesch.*, II : 295.

calls attention to the fact that divine illumination may relate to strictly supernatural matters, or may merely be designed to give perfect certainty concerning those things which the human mind can apprehend by its own unaided powers. The former is exemplified in the case of the authors of the Hagiographa, the latter in the prophets properly so called. The nearer to Christ the greater was the degree of illumination, until when Christ came the mystery of the Trinity was revealed. For this reason the writers of the New Testament rank higher than Moses.[1]

Revelation may be made in four ways: through *inward enlightenment*, which elevates the mental powers, through the *communication of ideas*, through *images of the imagination* and through the *perception of sensuous objects*, as e. g. the burning bush of Moses. Thomas does not appear to have regarded the activity of the Holy Spirit in inspiration as violent, or as crippling in any way the spontaneity of his human organs.

VIII. The Scholastics.

These theologians generally did little toward defining and developing the idea of inspiration. For the most part they accepted the traditional doctrine, assumed it as a first principle admitted by all, and made it a basis for further theological investigation. There seemed to be no need of proving, explaining or applying that which was unquestioned in the church.

IX. The Mystics.

The Mystics had naturally,— or at least should have had,— a keener sense of the divine wisdom and power displayed in the composition of the Scriptures, than the average Scholastic. To the Bible the more evangelical among them adhered, confessing it to be in some special sense the Word of God. Yet the truly Biblical idea of inspiration was obscured, if not wholly lost, for the great majority of them, by belief in the continued presence of this miraculous power in the church, and by confounding the nature of inspiration proper with that of divine illumination in general. Abstraction from the outward, close contemplation of

---

[1] Cremer, 753.

things eternal and divine,—even the immediate vision of the face of God was not only possible to man, but was the free privilege of him who would seek it in the way appointed. Divine visits and immediate revelations were esteemed matters of common experience among men of their own school of faith. They thus became objects of lawful desire and expectation. All this, indeed the whole grotesque and exaggerated conception of the supernatural in mediaeval Christianity, tended to obliterate the distinction between the immediate inspiration bestowed upon prophets and apostles, and the general enlightenment of ordinary believers.

Another tendency of Mysticism operated in the same direction. Absorption in God, loss of human will, desire and consciousness in the divine, of course meant the identification of man with God. Deity dwelt, it was said, within the recesses of the human spirit, and needed only to be roused to activity: every objective element in religion must retire before that which is subjective—what was this but pantheism, and that more than half-fledged? Not a few among the mystic sects went quite over, embracing pantheistic tenets in all their length and breadth. No doctrine of the inspiration of the Scriptures, it is plain, could find room here. There was nothing to distinguish it from the ravings of fanatical enthusiasm on the one hand, or the phenomena of human genius on the other.

Save in the development of a biblical tendency, mysticism contributed little to the growth and progress of the great doctrine with which we are concerned.

1. *Tauler.*

John Tauler († 1361), a noted evangelical mystic, has an utterance on inspiration which may be worth quoting, as relating to the extent of the divine influence upon the sacred writers in secular matters.[1]

"Did the disciple in the highest school of the Spirit obtain an insight into all those sciences which are learned in the school of nature? I answer 'Yes': it was given them to understand all science, whether touching the courses of the heavenly bodies or what not, in so far as it might conduce to God's glory, or con-

---

[1] But see *Tauler's Bekehrung von H. S. Denifle*; also review of same in *Presbyterian Review*, July, 1881.

cern the salvation of man; but those points of science which bear no fruits for the soul, they were not given to know."

X. Forerunners of the Reformation.

It is to those who are usually called 'forerunners of the Reformation' that we naturally look for the fullest, clearest and loftiest ideas of inspiration possible to this age. But our expectations are only partially realized.

1. *Wiclif.*

We search the writings of Wiclif († 1384) in vain for any extended formal discussion of the subject, though he published a treatise, '*Of the Truth of Holy Scripture.*' Bred to scholastic habits of thought, and to the acceptance of prevalent views respecting the two-fold source of Christian knowledge in reason and authority (which latter, nominally including Scripture, really meant ecclesiastical tradition), the reformer could work his way but slowly to that point where he could openly confess the exclusive and decisive divine authority of Scripture. He says that Scripture '*is* the word of God '—that 'it is the will and testament of God the Father, which cannot be broken '—and yet again that ' God and his word are one, and cannot be separated the one from the other'.[1] He declares Christ to be the proper author of Scripture, and infers from this fact its absolute authority. As Christ is infinitely superior to every other man, so is the book which is his law to every other writing which can be named.[2] He makes the Bible the supreme standard by which even the doctrines of the church-fathers are to be tried.

While missing, then, in Wiclif all abstract discussions of the question of inspiration, especially theorizings as to its nature or extent, we do see his ardent belief in the *fact* brought out, and the general complexion of his views. We are really at no loss to know where he stood.

2. *Savonarola.*

Savonarola († 1495) was orthodox in reference to our doctrine according to the idea of his time, though his opinions had a de-

---

[1] Lechler, *Life of Wiclif*, II : 19–20.
[2] Id., p. 20.

cidedly mystical tinge. He attributed unique inspiration to the Scriptures, but conceived that the energy and operation of the Holy Ghost were directed rather to impressing truth on the minds and hearts of his human organs, than to mechanical composition upon tables of stone or pieces of parchment. He held that the inspired writers retained their self-consciousness, spontaneity and other individual mental characteristics. He fell, however, into the common error of maintaining the *continuance* of inspiration, which he attributed, in the form of prophecy, to himself.

3. *John Wessel.*

Wessel (†1489), who was a contemporary of Savonarola, treats the question of inspiration at length, but in such a way as to show that his ideas were not free from confusion, especially as to the *nature* of the process. As Ullmann expresses it: "On the one hand, as he is convinced, a certain amount of imperfection cleaves to every human notion of revelation. The subject is never exhausted in the description; the substance always stretches beyond the form." "On the other hand, he adheres firmly to the strict notion of inspiration, and looks upon Scripture, both in its totality and in its minutest facts, as a thoroughly divine work."[1]

XI. The Jewish Doctrine.

The Jewish doctors of the Middle Ages sought to build up a theory of inspiration upon the foundation of the Talmud and Aristotelic philosophy. The tracing of its details is of no special importance to our immediate purpose. A few general statements will suffice.

Like the early Christian Apologists, and the contemporary Schoolmen, the Rabbins could conceive the doctrine only from the standpoint and under the typical form of *prophecy.* Their development of the same was marred by gross contradictions. They wavered notably in their idea of the

1. *Nature*

of the prophetic condition. Sometimes it was represented as one, not merely of pure passivity, but of absolute ecstasy in the strictest sense of the word.[2] Maimonides declares that every vision is

---

[1] *Reformers before the Reformation,* II : 420.
[2] Rudelbach, *Zeitsch. für die Gesammt. Luther. Theol., Zweit. Quart.,* 54.

accompanied with a state of panic terror, and that all the senses rest from their functions.¹ He quotes Daniel x : 8 ff. in proof of his assertion.

None the less was it maintained that the seer could exercise his office only in a calm and joyous frame of mind, because 'prophecy could not dwell amid confusion of the senses or pain, but only in the midst of joy.'¹

Rudelbach observes that both of these definitions must be taken as imperfect attempts to explain that which the Scripture embraces under the common name of prophecy.²

2. *Degrees.*

Various degrees of inspiration in prophecy were admitted. Maimonides attempted to determine them at 'eleven or eight,' of which the first two could only by a figure of speech be reckoned to the head of prophecy. Albo reduced these to four, and Abarbanel to three, corresponding to the three-fold division of the Jewish Scriptures into the Law, Prophets and Hagiographa.³ The Law embodied the highest stage of prophecy, and was the fountain-head of revelation; the Prophets ranked next, while the Hagiographa, being given not by the 'Spirit of prophecy,' but only by that of 'holiness,' could not be considered as in any real sense inspired at all.³

Maimonides (+1104), the only one of the later Jewish doctors whose opinion is of especial historical importance, far from conceding that the Bible was the pure product of the divine activity upon the human spirit, saw in it a book differing from other books, even on its religious side, not in kind, but only in degree. The mediaeval Spanish rabbi here shaped the thinking of the great Jewish pantheist of the seventeenth century, Spinoza, through him influenced the later German rationalism, and thus powerfully, though mediately, the English thought of our own age.

XII. General Conclusions.

If now we ask what is the significance of the Middle Ages, as a whole, for the history of our doctrine, it is hard to make answer.

---

[1] Maimon., *Moreh Nebuchim*, P. II., c. 41.

[2] *Zeitsch. für die Ges. Luth. Theol., Zw. Quart.*, 54.

[3] Rudelbach, *Zeitsch. &c.*, 57.

So far as progressive development is concerned, really nothing. In the general preparation for the Reformation, however, especially for the enunciation of its formal principle of the sole authority and sufficiency of the Scriptures as a rule of faith and practice—above all in the growth of the biblical factor in mysticism, we may trace the opening of the way for the subsequent definition, formulation and elevation of the doctrine to its proper place in the system of Protestant theology.

F. THE DOCTRINE OF INSPIRATION DURING THE REFORMATION ERA.

As Scholasticism left the idea of inspiration undeveloped, so the views of the leading reformers on the subject were in many respects indefinite. The matter did not come up for specific discussion, inasmuch as it did not form a subject of controversy with Rome. All parties agreed that the Scriptures of the Old and New Testament are the word of God, and authoritative in matters of faith and practice. Subordinate differences, however, did exist among the reformers in reference to the nature and extent of inspiration; and these appear, not as formally stated in express theories, but rather as incidentally developed in various utterances concerning the Holy Scriptures.

I. Erasmus.

It lay, as Kahnis admits,[1] in the very nature of Humanism, with all its emphasis of the biblical principle, to take a very free view of the human side of Scripture. Thus Erasmus (†1536) said: "Only Christ is free from error. The authority of Scripture is not destroyed if the sacred writers do sometimes disagree in word or meaning, provided only there remains unmoved the sum total of that upon which rests our salvation.

The divine Spirit who controlled the minds of the apostles suffered them to be ignorant of some things,—sometimes to mistake and err in judgment or affection, though never to the prejudice of the gospel."

This utterance he subsequently recalled.

---
[1] *Luther, Dogm.*, 1:274.

II. Luther.

The general attitude of Luther on the subject of inspiration was that of freedom, though in matters of detail it must be confessed that he stands in dogmatic contradiction with himself. All becomes clear only upon careful consideration, both of the man himself in his personal character and experience, and of the theologian, especially his views on the general doctrine of the Scriptures. This lies beyond our present purpose. We can attempt only the briefest outline of the subject immediately in question.

1. Luther calls the Bible 'the greatest and best book of God,' sees in it the 'living truth of the Holy Spirit,' and exalts it as 'the only source of knowledge of the pure apostolic word,' and as 'the only test and rule of the Christian life.'

2. He concedes a union of the divine and human factors in inspiration: and it is in this very distinction that one finds the secret of his two-fold and apparently inconsistent method of speaking of the Scriptures. The Holy Spirit, by his illuminating power, secured in the minds of the biblical writers all needful knowledge of divine truth, but this truth took on a human form, and thus became their inward personal possession. These writers made use of their own faculties in the attainment of historical knowledge, 'but they sifted it, arranged it, and set it in the true divine light by the power of the illuminating Spirit working in them.'[1] Thus Luther calls the books of Moses, 'writings of the Holy Ghost,' while he supposes that the legislator derived his laws from the traditional customs of the fathers of the Jewish nation. Of the prophets, he says: "Doubtless the prophets studied Moses, and the later prophets studied the earlier ones, and wrote down in a book their good thoughts inspired by the Holy Ghost."

All this goes to show that Luther entertained no mechanical view of inspiration, but held that the Holy Ghost made use of the human individuality of the Scripture writers as his free organs.[2]

3. As Luther insisted on the independence of faith with reference to the Scriptures, and demanded that it exercise the critical

---

[1] Dorner, *Mod. Prot., Theol.*, 1:255.

[2] Kahnis, *Luther. Dogm.*, 275.

office with regard to the canon, we are not surprised at the way in which he himself proceeded to the practical execution of the task.

He freely conceded the existence of imperfections and errors in the sacred records, arising either from undue haste, or from forgetfulness on the part of their authors: such, e. g., as Paul's use of the allegory of Hagar and Ishmael (Gal. 4:22), and Peter's allusion to Christ's preaching to the spirits in prison (1 Peter, 3:19). 'All in the Bible is not pure silver, gold and precious stones; one must look to find along with these hay, straw, stubble.' Still no harm is done, he thinks, provided only the foundation is well laid. This is always the main thing to be regarded.[1]

It may be well to notice (though not quite germane to our immediate subject), that Luther attributed very unequal value to different books of the Old and New Testaments. Of the former, he prized the Psalms most highly, while he rejected Esther and Ecclesiastes as uncanonical, declared the history of Jonah so monstrous as to be absolutely incredible, rated Chronicles as of inferior authority to Kings, thought that other books suffered revision by unknown hands, and doubted the Mosaic authorship of the Pentateuch.

In the New Testament, he assigned the chief rank to the gospel of John ('the one unique, tender, true, main gospel, far to be preferred to the others'), the Pauline epistles (especially those to the Romans, Galatians and Ephesians), and the First of Peter. The epistle of James, he designated as an 'epistle of straw,' 'with nothing evangelical about it,' because it exalts good works as related to faith. He felt the absence of the apostolic spirit in the epistle to the Hebrews, (which he attributed to Apollos,) and refused either an apostolic or prophetic character to the Apocalypse. He says: "I certainly cannot detect any trace of its having been inspired by the Holy Ghost."

He specifies certain books which he regards as the kernel and marrow of the sacred canon, because of their abundant testimony to Christ.

Witness to Christ, and not apostolic authorship is in his opinion the universal test of inspiration and canonicity. "What does not teach Christ, this is not apostolic even though Peter or

---

[1] Baur, *Dogm.-gesch.*, III: 60.

Paul teach it. And again, what teaches Christ, that is apostolic, even if Judas, Annas, Pilate and Herod teach it."[1]

We see from this that the critical spirit had been awakened in Luther's mind in reaction against the easy and unquestioning credulity of the church in which he had been trained. Although this spirit proceeded from and was governed by a living faith, rather than by a merely intellectual interest and curiosity, yet it was not sufficiently well instructed to restrain itself within due bounds.

4. To be at all consistent with himself, Luther should have resolutely rejected the strict theory of inspiration, which applied it to the form as well as to the substance—the words as well as the thoughts of the Scriptures. This he did in general. He would acknowledge no mechanical dictation of phraseology on the part of the inspiring Spirit to the sacred writers.

In his doctrine of the sacraments, however, he was compelled to contradict himself, and make everything dependent on word and letter. Here he found the Bible 'a book in which more depended on a single letter or a turn of the same, than on heaven and earth.'

5. It is evident, from what has already been said, that Luther admitted *degrees in inspiration*, which he determined according to the measure in which certain doctrines were more or less clearly, intelligibly and convincingly set forth.

III. Melancthon.

Heppe has said that no traces of a proper theory of inspiration are to be found in Melancthon. No inference, however, is to be drawn from this as to the doctrinal unsoundness of the reformer on this subject. He clearly taught the infallibility of the apostles in the *statement*, if not in the *application* of doctrinal truth.

IV. Zwingle.

Zwingle does not, in his writings, enter into detailed statements concerning the theory of inspiration. His views, however, while preserving some features in common with those of Luther, appear to have been much sounder, more churchly, and comparatively free from the exaggerations of a critical spirit. They were de-

---

[1] *Preface to Epistle of James.*

termined by the fact that in the Bible he found that rest from doubt and disquiet of conscience which he sought in vain from philosophy and scholasticism.

1. He held that the Scriptures are from God; that they contain the infallible revelation of his character and will, and form the only and sufficient source of knowledge in matters of faith, as well as an unerring rule in the conduct of daily life.

2. Like Luther, he seems to have conceded the existence of some distinction between the Scriptures and the word of God, finding the latter imbedded in the former like gold in the rock.

He admitted inaccuracies of historical statement in the Bible, and consequently could not predicate absolute infallibility of every writer on every subject. His words are as follows: "It is not true that the writings of all holy men are infallible; nor is it true that they do not err. This preëminence must be given to the Son of God alone, out of the whole human race."

This admission, however, did not interfere with the exalted estimate which he placed upon the Bible, or with the unique position which he assigned to it.

3. He denied the canonicity of the Apocalypse.

V. Calvin.

Calvin's views of inspiration were much stricter than those of either Luther or Zwingle, as he maintained approximately what is known as the 'plenary theory.' To mention some specific differences between Calvin and other reformers on the subject, we note:

1. He did not, like others, distinguish the form from the substance of Christian truth, but extended the influence of inspiration to both.

2. He refused to grant such free scope for the exercise of the critical spirit as Luther had done.

3. He gave preference to the *formal* over the *material* principle of the Reformation, i. e., dwelt more on the authority and sufficiency of the Scriptures than on the doctrine of justification by faith.

4. He extended the infallibility and authoritativeness of the Scriptures not only to matters of doctrine, but also to those of discipline and life. Hence his presbyterian church polity and theocratic civil government for Geneva.

Calvin calls God 'the author of the Scriptures,' notes their divine majesty, and speaks of the Holy Spirit who 'uttered his voice by the mouth of the prophets.' He attributes to the sacred records the same authority as though the 'living words of God were heard from heaven;' and yet unhesitatingly concedes slight inaccuracies and errors, e. g., in citations (Matt. 27:9). He also acknowledges the human element in the biblical writers, especially in their style. "Some prophets have a brilliant style, but by such the Holy Spirit wished to show that eloquence was not wanting to him, while elsewhere he made use of a rough and uncouth style."

Calvin confessed to certain critical scruples concerning the canonicity of the Second Epistle of Peter.

VI. Followers of the Great Reformers.

Among the immediate followers of the German and Swiss reformers, opinions were propounded implying somewhat free views of inspiration. Thus—

1. Bugenhagen (†1558) says incidentally: "Consider that the evangelists wrote each for himself what they saw, and oftentimes while they record what occurred, they are heedless of the *order* of occurrences."

2. Bullinger (†1575) writes in reference to 1 Cor. 10:8: "Transcribers easily fall into error in stating numbers; but sometimes the writers were also led by treacherous memories into the commission of mistakes."

VII. Remarks on Apparent Inconsistencies in the Attitude of the Reformers toward the Scriptures.

It is difficult to study the writings of the reformers without gaining the impression that their attitude toward the Holy Scriptures was in some sense anomalous and inconsistent. On the one hand, they declare them to be of divine origin, the word of God, the sole source and standard of all religious faith and practice, and, apart from tradition, themselves alone sufficient for salvation. On the other hand, *some* of the reformers at least allow themselves such freedom in the expression of critical opinion as seems incompatible with belief in the really supernatural inspiration of the Scriptures, their infallible truth and authoritativeness in the entire range of their contents. The apparent discrepancies of views and statements may be explained somewhat as follows:

1. The hierarchical church for centuries exerted herself to the utmost to suppress all independence and individuality of thought, all close investigation of the *substance* of religious truth, and especially all study of the Scriptures. By unsparing use of the powers at her command—penalties civil and ecclesiastical, terrors temporal and eternal—she in the main succeeded in her aim. As the human mind, however, must have some field for its activities, she graciously permitted a measure of freedom in dealing with the *forms* of faith. Theologians, if first supremely loyal to the church, and submissive to her arbitrary restraints upon learning, might take the material which she provided and work upon it. They might define, systematize, demonstrate and defend ancient ecclesiastical dogmas—in short, might justify to reason what had first been received by faith. This produced the scholastic theology which rose, culminated, declined and died a natural death before the time of Luther.

But if the system itself had passed away, the spirit which it nurtured, its methods and many of its most untoward efforts remained. Among these none was more disastrous than that of a subtle and acute, but superficial and cold questioning of the forms of truth—*forms*, we say, for it lacked the vitality to go below the surface to the deep reality of things.

When now the Revival of Letters opened up the treasures of classical antiquity, the sources of early Christian history, and the Scriptures themselves in their original tongues, then under the impulse inspired by Humanism, this same critical spirit, furnished with a new and worthy object, turned its attention to the whole church-system 'from turret to foundation stone.' Not only was the real character of the existing theology exposed to view, but the sources of that theology in Scripture and ecclesiastical tradition were subjected to rigid scrutiny. *One* idol of infallibility was at once destroyed, and the sceptical Humanism was not slow to ask whether a fallible element might not exist within the *other*. Not only did the Reformation movement itself in general tend to boldness of thought and freedom of inquiry, but this critical spirit, roused in reaction against the unquestioning credulity of 'mother-church,'—eager, self-confident, but not half instructed, knew not to restrain itself within due bounds; but, in regard to problems presented by the Holy Scriptures, often jumped at conclusions from questionable premises, especially if thereby a blow might be dealt at the hierarchy and the traditional system it supported.

We do not forget that in Germany the new studies were prosecuted in a more religious spirit than elsewhere, and that literature ultimately became the handmaid of religion; neither do we claim that the spirit above described was at all that in which the reformers consciously approached the Scriptures; but we do claim that this was the atmosphere in which they grew up, and the school in which they had their training. It was not possible, humanly speaking, that they should wholly escape its influence in forming judgment of the Bible (then first made accessible), whether regard was had to its character and contents, or the influences under which it was composed.

2. On the other hand, we must give due weight to the part which *mysticism* played, not only in preparation for the Reformation in general, but especially in determining the views of the reformers with reference to the written word of God. Its influence was two-fold—helpful and harmful. It led its adherents—

a. From the abstruse, barren speculations of the schools to personal, spiritual life.

b. In its later stages, from tradition to Scripture. As the practical and biblical factors in mysticism were developed, the circulation of the Bible and of religious writings among the laity was widely extended.

c. From dependence on outward works, and faith in sacraments and ceremonies, to attention to the inward spirit and the motives which govern conduct, and to direct approach to Christ and the Holy Spirit.

d. From sermonizing in the traditional Latin, on the legends of the saints, the story of the Trojan war, and like themes, to preaching in the vernacular the doctrine of salvation by Christ.

None the less was mysticism defective (as seen in its operations during the Middle Ages) in overestimating the subjective, and underrating the objective element in religion. It regarded what Christ does *in* us rather than *for* us, and overlooked the necessity and unique divinity of the *written word*, while it exalted the 'inward light,' the personal dealings of the Holy Ghost with believers—indeed practically deified humanity. Mysticism had, it is true, been purified in proportion to the development of its biblical factor, but its (in measure at least untoward) influence upon the reformers, especially upon Luther, Zwingle and others is not only traceable outwardly, but is clearly proved by internal evidence. Example is seen in the tendency of these men to judge of Holy Scripture according to a standard purely subjective— what it had done for them in personal experience, rather than by any objective test whatever. From this point of view, defects as well as excellencies were freely predicated of that which after all their hearts embraced and treasured as God's most precious gift to man.

Of course nothing here said will be interpreted as hinting that the reformers ever *intended* to question the supernatural inspiration of the Scriptures, deny to them supreme authority as the court of last appeal in matters of doctrine, or regard them as other than the infallible standard of perfect rectitude of life. No Christian teachers in any age, not even the advocates of the most rigid theory of mechanical inspiration, ever so exalted the dignity and glory of the Word as did the great leaders of Christian thought and life in the sixteenth century. It is simply hoped that the suggestions given may throw some light upon that which has often otherwise seemed anomalous and unaccountable.

G. THE DOCTRINE OF INSPIRATION DURING THE SEVENTEENTH CENTURY.

I. Lutheran.

It was, partially at least, a polemic interest and tendency that led to the abandonment of the generally free view of inspiration held by the early reformers, and the development of those extreme ideas, especially in the Lutheran theology of the seventeenth century, which wholly suppressed the human element in the composition of the sacred records, and attributed to their contents a mechanical, literal divinity. Luther's free view had been abused by the church of Rome to the furtherance of her doctrine of the insufficiency and obscurity of the Scriptures, and of the authority and supremacy of ecclesiastical tradition. Protestant orthodoxy, however, asserted itself with vigor, not only against Romanists, but also against Arminians, Socinians and Mystics. The material here is so abundant as to forbid the presentation of the views of individual theologians in detail. It must be arranged under a few specific heads:

1. *The Nature of Inspiration.*

a. Authorship.

The theologians of this school taught that God is the only real author of Scripture. As Quenstedt († 1688) says: "God alone, if we wish to speak accurately, should be called the author of sacred Scripture." Of the persons of the Trinity, it is the Holy Ghost to whom inspiration pertains as part of his especial economic functions. He, however, did not write immediately, but made use of the sacred penmen. He therefore is the primary Author, they the secondary authors.[1]

The relation of inspired men to the inspiring Spirit was conceived as purely passive. From the latter only proceeded the impulse to write, and in the process of writing itself, men could rank only as 'the pens or the amanuenses of the Holy Ghost.'[2]

Thus Gerhard († 1637) says: "The efficient, principal cause of sacred Scripture is God; the instrumental causes were holy men. They wrote not as men, but as men of God; i. e., servants of God and special organs of the Holy Ghost."[3]

Again: "One may rightly call the apostles and prophets amanuenses of God, hands of Christ, and notaries or secretaries of the Holy Ghost, since they spoke or wrote nothing according to their own human will. All therefore was suggested and inspired within them."[4]

Quite in the same strain, Quenstedt labors to define the nature of the state of passivity in which the sacred writers fulfilled their functions, and says that they wrote nothing 'out of their own understanding, but all things under the direction of the Holy Ghost.'

The Lutheran divines conceived it as quite natural that in considering the origin of any particular book of Scripture, the sec-

---

[1] Kahnis, *Luther. Dogm.*, 279.
[2] Baur, *Dogm.-gesch.*, III : 61.
[3] Gerhard, *Loci.* I, c. 12, § 12.
[4] *Explic. über Loc.* I, c. 2, § 18.

ondary author should be wholly overlooked, and attention exclusively directed to the primary Author, the divine Originator.

b. Act of Inspiration.

According to the same theologians, the act of inspiration by the Holy Ghost included three things: the impulse to write [i. e., the mere mechanical operation of writing, for as Hollaz († 1713) says: "The words were inspired within the prophets, not to be understood, but to be written"], the suggestion of the matter, and that of the words.

Thus Baier (†1695) defines inspiration as "an act of that kind by which God supernaturally communicated to the intellect of the writers, not only the ideas of all things which were to be recorded, but also of the words themselves, and of all things by which they should be expressed; and then roused the will to the act of writing."[1]

Quenstedt says again: "All and everything which is contained in the Holy Scriptures, whether in the natural way wholly unknown, or naturally, indeed, capable of being known, but actually unknown; or yet again, not only naturally apprehensible, but also actually known, either from personal experience or from some other source—all this was not merely written by means of infallible divine assistance and direction, but flowed from the special suggestion, inspiration and dictation of the Spirit. For all which was to be written, was suggested by the Holy Ghost to the sacred writers in the act of writing, and was dictated to their understanding as to a pen, so that it must be set down in writing with these and no other conditions, in this and no other way."

It is easily seen that this method of conceiving inspiration established a real Docetism, through the sole activity of the divine Spirit, and the annihilation of all human spontaneity.

c. Revelation and Inspiration.

A distinction was made between *revelation* and *inspiration*, though it was not always kept clear and exact. It was taught that the former relates properly to the communication of truth before unknown, and may be made in various ways and for various purposes. The latter relates by right only to the act of writing,

---

[1] *Compendium*, p. 65.

concerns either that which was previously hidden or already disclosed, and is effected only through the Holy Ghost.¹

Another distinction made by theologians of more liberal views will be noticed below.

2. *The Extent of Inspiration.* (*Verbal Inspiration.*)

a. Citations already made show clearly the views of the High Lutheran theologians of the seventeenth century in the matter. Everything pertaining to Scripture, whether substance or form, was alike the direct work of the Holy Ghost. Prophecy, dogma, poetry, history,—all, without exception, were included.

Thus Quenstedt: "The original Scripture is of infallible truth, and free from every error; or what is the same thing, in canonical Scripture there is no falsehood, no untruth, not even the least error either in facts or in words; but all things and everything which is related there, is most true, whether those things are doctrinal, moral, historical, chronological or topographical, and no ignorance, thoughtlessness or forgetfulness, no error of memory can be, or ought to be, imputed to the amanuenses of the Holy Ghost in their records."

Words as well as things were included. Calovius (†1686) declared that, 'God inspired those things which apostles and prophets wrote, and not only as to the sense and meaning, but as to the words which were suggested and dictated to them, just as they are contained in Scripture.'

Hollaz: "All words and every word which is contained in the sacred text was inspired by the Holy Spirit in prophets and apostles, and was dictated to a pen."

Quenstedt: "The words themselves, and all and every expression has the Holy Ghost individually suggested, inspired, and dictated to the sacred writers."

b. The Lutheran theologians maintained that the Hebrew vowel points were original, rather than the work of the later Massoretes, and thus partook of the inspiration of the text.

Gerhard said that to deny that the vowels and points of the Old Testament proceeded from inspiration would compel one to deny the doctrine of verbal inspiration wholly.

---

¹ Kahnis, *Luther. Dogm.*, 1:279. Baur, *Dogm.-gesch.*, III:60.

Calovius supported the same theory by the declaration that 'not one jot or tittle should in any wise pass from the Law.'
Similarly speak Quenstedt and Hollaz.

It thus appears, to speak briefly, that the Lutheran divines of this period regarded every *word* and every *letter* of the Scriptures as the *direct utterance and work of the Holy Ghost.*

3. *Objections Answered.*

It could hardly escape the notice of these Protestant scholastics that the views propounded and defended by them encountered many difficulties, and were liable to serious objections; but theological ingenuity and acuteness were then, as always, ready with a plausible answer.

a. When it was asked how on this basis the evident differences of style among the sacred writers were to be accounted for, Calovius said plainly: "The cause of different methods of expression is that the Holy Spirit makes each one to speak just as he wishes.[1]

Quenstedt and Hollaz point to the manifoldness of the contents of the Scripture which, they say, demands a corresponding variety of style. They also assume an accommodation on the part of the Holy Ghost to the individual peculiarities of the sacred writers,[2] making him thereby the cleverest of imitators.

A somewhat fuller form of reply to this objection was that the Holy Ghost, as the Lord of all gifts of utterance, could speak as he would, and vary his style according to his pleasure. In dictating to each sacred writer, he chose just such methods of expression as that person would have chosen had he been writing under a voluntary impulse. So carefully did the divine author adapt himself to the individuality and the grade of culture of each one.

b. To the charge of barbarisms or solecisms in style, a flat denial was returned.

Hollaz declares: "The style of the sacred Scriptures is dignified, worthy of the divine Majesty, and is disfigured by no grammatical fault, by no barbarism or solecism. To maintain the contrary is blasphemy."

---

[1] *Syst.* I., p. 574.
[2] Kahnis, *Luther. Dogm.*, 281.

4. More Liberal Views.

A few Lutheran theologians had the courage to array themselves against the doctrinal exaggerations of their contemporaries, though the result was to draw upon themselves the charge of unsoundness in the faith, and even the accusation of positive heresy. Chief among them were Musaeus and Calixtus.

a. Musaeus († 1681) ventured to express doubts whether inspiration extended to the words as well as to the matter of the Scriptures. He even designated verbal inspiration as an undecided and improbable opinion. But for this hardihood he was violently opposed by the zealous orthodox divines, especially by Calovius, and was compelled to retract his utterances.

b. Calixtus († 1656) wished to distinguish between *revelation* or *inspiration in the strict sense*, and mere *divine assistance*. To the former he would ascribe only the chief doctrines of the Scriptures, viz., those relating to human redemption and final salvation. For other things which might be learned from the light of nature or through experience, he claimed only that divine assistance which guarded the sacred writers from error, and enabled them to record that which was 'consonant with fact, true, worthy and suitable.' For these too free views Calixtus found himself charged with heresy.[1]

5. The Lutheran Symbols.

The silence of the Lutheran symbolic books respecting inspiration has often been remarked. The explanation seems to be that the *fact* is presupposed, while, for various reasons, implied in what has been said above, no specific *theory* is proposed. Incidental expressions are found in the Apology, in the Smalcald Articles, and in the Formula of Concord, which confirm this view.

II. Reformed.

The Reformed churches of the continent were generally in harmony with the Lutheran in their doctrine of sacred Scripture. Within the former a somewhat animated controversy was carried on respecting the inspiration of the vowel-points of the Hebrew text. The principal disputants were the two Buxtorffs, father

---

[1] Baur, *Dogm.-gesch.*, III: 63.

(† 1639) and son († 1664), professors at Basle, on the one side, and Leo Capellus on the other. The former asserted both the antiquity and divine origin of the vowel-points, as essential to any true doctrine of inspiration. The latter claimed them as a later growth upon the text, and appealed, in confirmation of his view, to both Jewish and Christian testimonies. The orthodox opinion was finally confirmed and formulated in the *Formula Consensus Helvetici* (1675), which declares that 'not only the consonants, but also the vowels—either the points themselves, or at least the meaning of the points—were inspired by God.'

It is undeniable, however, that some divines in the Reformed churches entertained less rigid views. This was particularly true of the French theologians of the school of Saumur, who could admit, e. g., without scruple, that the New Testament writers had misapprehended the meaning of those of the Old, or had fallen into errors of memory.

German Reformed theologians also, like Junius Piscator and others, were in like manner inclined to liberal views. In both the French and Swiss Reformed churches the radical and rationalistic views of Le Clerc generally found wide and welcome reception. Pictet, e. g., professor at Geneva in 1702, taught that inspiration in Scripture was limited to those truths which men can attain only by the aid of revelation proper. The revelation, of course, never extended to matter knowable by means of the natural faculties. For these, divine guidance in preventing errors was amply sufficient.

III. Roman Catholic.

A reaction against the exaggerated orthodoxy and extreme literalism of the Protestant theologians was inevitable, and actually appeared in various quarters. We notice first the Roman Catholics.

1. The Canons of Trent incidentally refer to the Scriptures as a 'dictation of the Holy Ghost,' but determine nothing otherwise concerning the theory of inspiration. Ecclesiastical opinion, however, practically declared that the Scriptures and their authority were dependent upon and subordinate to the authority of the church.

2. Bellarmine († 1620) contended that the original commission

of the apostles concerned preaching and not writing; that their epistles were merely occasional letters, and did not fundamentally affect doctrine.[1] He maintained that the sacred penmen formed the determination to write from existing circumstances, and attributed to God such a direction or assistance only as allowed the preservation of their spontaneity. He made a broad distinction between the prophetic and historical writers, holding that the kind of aid rendered to each was different, and adapted to their needs. He says: "God aided the prophets in one way, and the historical writers in another. To the former he revealed the future, and assisted them so that nothing false should mingle with what they wrote. To the latter he did not always reveal what they should write, but only stirred them up to write what they had seen and heard and remembered. At the same time he helped them not to write anything false; but this assistance did not exclude labor on their part."[2]

All this indicates a disposition to limit the province of immediate inspiration as much as possible.

3. Several of the most learned papal doctors were inclined to limit strict inspiration to the essential articles of faith,[3] and to maintain that in other matters, e. g., historical narratives, the sacred writers were left to themselves, and might sometimes err. Pighius says boldly: "Matthew and John were able to err in memory, and to falsify." The Jesuits were especially loose in their views, and were ready to concede the fallibility of prophets and apostles. For this, however, they were condemned in 1586 by the faculties of Louvain and Douai.

Critical investigations upon the canon and the doctrine of inspiration were actually instituted during this period, and were perhaps mainly possible in the Catholic church. Those of Richard Simon were especially famous, and did much to impair belief in the divinity and canonical authority of the books of the Bible, especially of the Old Testament.[4] His opinions were certainly inconsistent with the acceptance of the theory of verbal and literal inspiration. He taught that inspiration should be viewed as

---

[1] Kahnis, *Luther. Dogm.*, I: 277.

[2] *De Verb. Div.*, I: 18.

[3] Haag, *Hist. des Dogm.*, I: 11.

[4] Id. ib.

an act of divine Providence, by which the sacred writers were in general directed, and were preserved from dangerous errors. This and nothing more. The learned Oratorian remarked that 'it was for Protestants only to fear and take offense at the results of criticism. Catholics could have no such scruples, because their faith did not depend merely on the sacred text.'[1]

IV. Arminian.

The Arminians shared the Catholic breadth and looseness of view respecting our doctrine, though from another point of view, in the interest of reason rather than of the church. The *tendency* was to limit the field of inspiration still further, though in their doctrinal system and public writings they did not oppose the current ecclesiastical doctrine. Looseness of view among the Arminians was greatly promoted by intercourse and connection with the Socinians.

1. Limborch († 1712) expressed himself concerning the question only with the greatest caution, saying that 'as the apostles, under the impulse of the Holy Ghost, set about their task, so also in writing they were so far directed that they could commit no error either in expressing the sense itself, or in recording the words which expressed the divine sense.'[2]

Other theologians showed themselves less timid.

2. Grotius († 1645) would concede inspiration, in the proper sense of the term, to the prophetic writings alone, but wholly denied it in the case of the historical books, refusing to put them in the same category, on the ground that historical narrative needed no inspiration. His exact words are these: "Not all books which are in the Hebrew canon were dictated by the Holy Spirit. I do not deny that they were written with pious intent, but there was no need that histories should be dictated by the Holy Ghost. It was enough that the writer had a clear recollection of the things seen."[3]

He specifies the writings of Luke as an example: "If Luke recorded only what the Holy Ghost dictated to him, why did he

---

[1] Baur, *Dogm.-gesch.*, III: 65.

[2] *Theol. Christ.*, Lib. I, cap. IV.

[3] *Votum pro Pace Ecclesiast.*

make appeal to his investigations?"¹ Grotius conceded the canonicity of Luke's writings, but only on the ground that in the opinion of the primitive church they 'are true, pious, and treat of important subjects.'²

3. Episcopius († 1643) goes still further, and says that the sacred writers might readily err, since in historical and related kinds of composition, for which the unaided human faculties were sufficient, they were left wholly to themselves. To the objection that on this basis they might err even in essential things, he replies that God did not entrust matters of great moment to human weakness, but reserved them to his own guidance and control.³

He argues also against the strict view of inspiration, that many books of Scripture either contain nothing which others had not given in greater detail, or at least are not especially edifying. Mention is also made of the fact that the so-called canonical writings were not collected in obedience to express divine command.⁴

4. Le Clerc († 1737), one of the most learned theologians of his age, held that genuine divine revelation renders inspiration needless. The prophecies themselves were communicated by revelation to the prophets, who carefully remembered them, but recorded them, each in his own style, so that it could not be said that they repeated the very words which they had heard.⁵

The historical books require no inspiration, and prove their actual want of the same by internal contradictions.⁶ Equally unnecessary is the supposition of inspiration in the case of the doctrinal books of the Old Testament; and as for the New Testament, the '*assistance*' of the Holy Ghost was amply sufficient for all purposes.

Christ had promised that the 'Spirit of the Father' should speak through the disciples (Matt. 10:20), but this he interpreted to refer to the spirit of holiness and steadfastness with which they would endure persecutions, and defend their doctrine.

---

[1] *Votum pro Pace Ecclesiast.*

[2] Baur, *Dogm.-gesch.*, III, 65.

[3] *Institutiones*, IV:1, 4.

[4] Id. IV:1, 4. Kahnis, *Luther. Dogm.*, I:278.

[5] *Sentiments de Quelques Theol. de Hollande*, &c. Haag, *Hist. des Dogm.*, I:12.

[6] Kahnis, *Luther. Dogm.*, 279. Baur, *Dogm.-gesch.*, III:4, 21.

The promise that the Spirit should 'guide the disciples into all truth, &c.,' (John 16:13,) was explained as teaching that divine aid would be given to strengthen the memory, and make needed explanations of truth. The apostles did not claim inspiration or deem it necessary to the validity of the doctrinal contents of their writings.

The views of Le Clerc here had much in common with those of Spinoza.

It thus appears that the Arminian view of inspiration implied a great relaxation of the strictness of the general Protestant church doctrine; among other things, greatly widening the field of spontaneity and conscious personal activity on the part of the sacred writers.

V. Socinian.

The Socinians did not by any means deny the *fact* of inspiration, but were otherwise grossly inconsistent in their views. The Racovian Catechism (preface) teaches that 'the Holy Ghost dictated the matter of Scripture to the apostles, and sometimes the very words, so that they were his mere instruments.' Inspiration is conceived as the immediate and coërcive operation of an outside Power upon the sacred writers, rather than the inter-penetration of their personality by a higher Influence, and thus the self-conscious elevation of their human faculties to apprehend the divine truth and will. Socinianism here occupies common ground with High Lutheran and Reformed orthodoxy.

1. Faustus Socinus himself confesses that the authors of Scripture wrote 'under the impulse of the divine Spirit and at his dictation,'[1] yet he elsewhere says that the 'natural abilities of the New Testament writers were abundantly sufficient for the communication of doctrine,' under which he would include only the most weighty practical truths.[2] He limits inspiration to essential things, and admits without scruple slight errors of memory, which do not in any way affect the truth of the sacred narrative. Socinus has no hesitation in exalting the New Testament above the Old, and in declaring that 'the reading of the latter, while useful, is by no means necessary.'

---

[1] *Lectiones Sacrae*, p. 287.

[2] *De Auc. S. Script.*, c. 4. Baur, *Dogm.-gesch.*, III:65.

To the Socinians the *inspiration* of the Bible was a question quite subordinate in importance to that of its human and historic *credibility*, and the divinity of written words was of far less moment than that of the general Christian faith and order. They came to feel less and less concern about difficulties and apparent discrepancies in Scripture, and were inclined to cut and clip it according to their own subjective ideas of reason and common sense. The ever growing looseness of view among these sectaries was coincident with, and based upon the ever increasing breadth of province and number of functions assigned to reason in its relation to Revelation.

VI. Mystic.

The mystics of the seventeenth century, as those of the Reformation era and other periods, tended to exalt unduly the teaching of the illuminating Spirit, and to disparage the value of the written Word. The Scriptures were treated very generally as a merely subordinate revelation, and sometimes as a detriment to that inward revelation which alone is true and immediate. Thus—

1. Christian Hoburg said: "Scripture is an old, cold and dead thing, which makes men mere Pharises."

2. Arndt: "Christ is the living book in whom we read, and from whom we should learn."

3. Weigel: "Scripture, as such, is a dead letter, and an empty word which sounds through the air."

4. *Fox.*

George Fox († 1691), founder of the sect of Quakers, declared: "It is not the Scriptures, but the Holy Spirit by which opinions and religions are to be tried."

5. *Barclay.*

Robert Barclay († 1690), the principal theologian of the same denomination, taught that 'Holy Writ is not the original source of knowing the truth; it is no adequate rule for doctrines and morals. * * * It is subordinate to the Holy Spirit, from whom it derives its excellence.'

Even when the Bible was nominally received and confessed as

authoritative, ideas were often ascribed to its divine Author, the Holy Ghost, which in reality were only the products of a morbid and enthusiastic fancy.

Spener († 1705), observing the reaction setting in among the orthodox divines in favor of exaggerated notions of literal inspiration, endeavored to mediate between the two parties, and on the true Protestant principle, reconcile the teaching of the inward Spirit with the authority of the written Word. His effort was to enhance the value placed upon the Bible both by the people and the theologians.[1]

In his personal views he confesses, with the mystics, that the mere letter of Scripture is powerless and dead; but against them he declares that, 'our feelings are not the norm of truth, but divine truth is the norm of our feelings. The rule of truth exists in the divine word, apart from ourselves.'[2]

With equal earnestness did he oppose the dead mechanism of church orthodoxy, and maintain the independence of the Scripture writers. He says: "Assuredly the things the apostles wrote, they understood, and did not produce sounds like parrots. But the understanding demands its own images or ideas which it forms, drawing them either from within or from some other source."[3]

VII. Opinion in England.

Public opinion was not so generally or profoundly stirred upon the question of inspiration either among the churchmen or dissenters of England, as among the Lutheran and Reformed churches of the Continent. Still the subject was not without interest, and some opinions were expressed which are worthy of record.

1. *Archbishop Tillotson.*

This prelate († 1694) hesitated to declare himself frankly respecting the *extent* of inspiration. He is not sure whether the divine superintendence merely secured the Scripture writers

---

[1] Hagenbach, *Hist. Doct.*, II : 246.

[2] Beck, *Dogm.-gesch.*, 120.

[3] *Consil. Theol.*, I : 45.

against error in the delivery of doctrine and narration of fact, while each was left to his own style and manner of expression; or, whether everything written was immediately dictated, words and phrases as well as sense, so that human authors were merely the penmen or instruments of the Spirit. He is only clear that the measure of inspiration was in every case sufficient to secure the end of Scripture, viz., to inform the world of the mind and will of God.[1]

He is *inclined* to think that Moses wrote the account of that in which he was personally concerned without immediate revelation; that Solomon, by natural and acquired wisdom, might utter his sententious Proverbs; that the evangelists might record what they saw and heard, or learned from others; that Paul might make certain local allusions contained in his epistles without immediate dictation. He finds *probable* argument for this view, e. g., in the verbal disagreements combined with the substantial harmony of the Evangelists, in the various readings of the Old and New Testaments, &c.[2] He finally, though with apparent hesitation, concludes that the Spirit of God did reveal to the penmen of the Scriptures what was necessary to be revealed; and as to all other things, that he did secure them from any material error or mistake in what they have delivered.

Not very profound or venturesome utterances for the Archbishop of Canterbury and Primate of all England.

2. *Burnet.*

Burnet, bishop of Salisbury († 1715), argues that inspiration left the sacred writers to the use of their own faculties, and to their previous customs and habits. The object of God was to give such representations of matters of fact as might work upon and affect belief. The order of time and strict words, not affecting this end, might vary according to occasion.

As to the doctrinal part, i. e., the rules of life given, or the propositions laid down, all must acquiesce in them as the voice of God. The explanations or arguments supporting these may be of various value, and are to be estimated according to their intrinsic

---

[1] Works, vol. IX: 233.
[2] Id., 234.

character. Burnet says, expressly: "When the divine writers argue upon any point, we are always bound to believe the conclusions that their reasonings end in, as parts of divine revelation; but we are not bound to be able to make out, or even to assent to all the premises made use of by them in their whole extent; unless it appears plainly that they affirm the premises as expressly as they do the conclusions proved by them."[1]

3. *Baxter.*

Richard Baxter († 1691), among the dissenting divines of England in the seventeenth century, is noteworthy for his somewhat latitudinarian position on the question before us. He would limit inspiration to the subject-matter of Scripture. He says: "The Scripture is like a man's body, where some parts are but for the preservation of the rest, and may be maimed without death. The sense is the soul of Scripture, and the letters but the body or vehicle. The doctrine of the Creed, Lord's Prayer, and Decalogue is the vital part, and Christianity itself. The Old Testament letter (written as we have it about Ezra's time) is that vehicle, which is as imperfect as the Revelation of these times was. But as after Christ's incarnation and ascension, the Spirit was more abundantly given, and the Revelation more perfect and sealed, so the doctrine is more full, and the vehicle or body, that is, are less imperfect and more sure to us; so that he that doubteth of the truth of some words in the Old Testament, or of some circumstances in the New, hath no reason to doubt therefore of the Christian religion, of which these doctrines are but the vehicle or body, sufficient to ascertain of the truth of the History and Doctrine."[2]

4. *John Owen.*

Very different from the attitude of Baxter was that occupied by the Puritan divine, John Owen († 1683), who was quite in accord upon this subject with the Lutheran and Reformed scholastics of the Continent, and may be taken as an example of the extremely rigid views prevalent among most of the contemporary

---

[1] Burnet on the Thirty-nine Articles, 112.
[2] *The Catechizing of Families*, 1683, p. 36.

Puritans in England. He treats inspiration from the standpoint of prophecy, and makes it, on the divine side, to be "an act of the Holy Ghost in communicating his mind to the prophets."[1] From this point of view three things enter into it:

a. The inspiration of the minds of holy men with the knowledge and apprehension of the things communicated to them.

b. The suggestion of words to express what their minds conceived.

c. The guidance of their hands in setting down the words suggested.

If either of these requisites were wanting, the Scriptures could not be absolutely and every way divine and infallible.[2]

As to the *extent* of inspiration, he observes: "It is not enough to satisfy us that the doctrines mentioned are preserved entire: every tittle and iota of the word of God must come under our consideration as being as such from God."

Again: "The Scriptures of the Old and New Testaments were immediately and entirely given out by God himself, his mind being in them represented to us without the least interveniency of such mediums and ways as were capable of giving change or alteration of the least letter or syllable."

Careful study shows that he intended to reject, and perhaps with equal emphasis, two opposite errors: one, that the matter only of the Holy Scripture was divinely communicated, while the verbal expression was left to the natural faculties; and the other, that the minds of the sacred penmen were under such coercive influence from above that they became mere machines. All used their own intellects and powers, and the Holy Spirit suggested such words as were familiar to each, but yet in such way that the words fixed upon were from him as directly and certainly as if they had been spoken to them by an audible voice."[3]

---

[1] Works, Carter's edition, III: 131.
[2] Id., 144.
[3] Id., 145.

H. THE DOCTRINE OF INSPIRATION DURING THE EIGHTEENTH CENTURY.

The ultra-orthodox doctrine of inspiration affirmed by the Lutheran and Reformed scholastics of the seventeenth century was during the succeeding one greatly modified and limited,—in many quarters, wholly abrogated. Some powerful specific agencies were at work to produce these radical changes. Among them may be mentioned on the one side, the influence of Spinoza and his philosophic system, as well as that of English Deism; on the other, the rise of Pietism. Each contributed in its own way and measure. But more than this: the old theories seemed to come in conflict with almost every aspect of the progressive thought of the eighteenth century, and were outlawed by reason of the difficulties and contradictions in which they involved their advocates, as well as by the positive advance in criticism, exegesis and philosophy. The real attack on the strict Lutheran doctrine began about the end of the seventeenth century, and took two main directions, a historic and a philosophic. The former concerned the doctrine of inspiration in general, and its practical application to specific books and passages; the latter extended to revelation as well as inspiration, and partook rather of a philosophic and dogmatic character.[1] The one kind was determined, as just indicated, by the progress both of criticism and interpretation, as well as by that of historical theology in general. Most important here was Semler, who really inaugurated the revolutionary epoch in German theology.[2]

Attacks of the second sort were probably at least an indirect result of the influence of the writings of Spinoza, while they were greatly furthered by the aid of the Kantian philosophy and its application to theology.[3] Each in its way contributed powerfully not only to the overthrow of old ideas, but to the development of a freer philosophical interpretation of the idea and theory of inspiration.

As the result of the coworking of all influences there followed a notable reconstruction of the doctrine. Henceforward inspira-

---

[1] Münscher, *Dogm.-gesch.* (Neudecker), II: 2, 239.
[2] Rudelbach, *Zeitsch. für die Gesammt. Luther. Theol.*, 1840, Zweit. Quart., 58.
[3] Münscher, *ut sup.*

tion, even among divines of reputed orthodoxy, was conceived not in an isolated way, but as standing in organic union with the collective mental and spiritual life of the sacred writers. It was referred chiefly to the kernel of saving truth, and to other contents of Scripture only according to the measure of their connection with this.[1] Distinctions of degree in inspiration were also conceded, German theologians in general no longer maintaining the universal and absolute infallibility of all details of the sacred records.

Accurate grouping of the various views that now demand our notice is by no means an easy task. We may, however, begin with—

I. The Rationalistic.

1. *Pfaff.*

Pfaff († 1760) was among the earliest Lutheran theologians who, in his treatment of the doctrine, betrayed a clear tendency to a radical departure from rigid and traditional views. He distinguished different degrees in inspiration.

a. *Immediate revelation*, made to the apostles and other writers of the New Testament concerning matters either wholly or in part unknown before.

b. *Immediate direction*, in the setting forth of parts which were known to them before, as also in the development of doctrine.

c. *Divine permission* in presenting those things which required neither 'revelation' nor 'immediate guidance.'

This last and lowest degree was consistent with purely human ideas.

2. *Töllner.*

Töllner published in 1772 a treatise entitled 'Die göttliche Eingebung der heiligen Schrift,' which constitutes one of the most important works for the history of inspiration during this period. He sought to show that the doctrine in question is not so vital to Christianity as commonly supposed. Revealed religion does not stand or fall with the divine inspiration of a book, and

---

[1] Lechler, *Dogm.-gesch.*

excessive regard for the mere letter of Scripture must involve one in continual doubt and perplexity, through the progress of criticism and general science.¹ Having proved, as he thinks, by historic evidence that the freer view of inspiration has been the controlling one in every age, Töllner proceeds to the execution of his main purpose, adopting therfor and making rigorous use of the analytic method. The chief peculiarities of his view may be thus briefly summed up :

a. There are five degrees of inspiration, and the differentiating element in each is the measure of the supernatural divine coöperation. These degrees he analyses and distinguishes with philosophical precision, though without attempting to decide what special degree is found in a given passage of Scripture.

b. The divine authority of the Bible is ensured even without inspiration.

c. Inspiration is a 'mere synergism,' or an assistance of the Holy Spirit, through which the sacred writers were preserved from error, and were enabled to compose their writings in a manner consonant with the end in view.

d. A broad distinction is to be made between the Scriptures and the word of God.

It need scarcely be said that the general results of Töllner's investigatio s in this department were wholly favorable to *negative* criticism.

3. *Semler.*

Semler († 1791), founder of the School of so-called 'historical biblical criticism,' took for his point of departure, *morality*, or *general utility* as constituting the essential character of the *divine*, since it facilitates spiritual goodness in mankind.² Moral improvement, therefore, is the essence of all religion. The Spirit of Christ is nothing else than the living apprehension and exhibition of moral truth in the fulness of its divine extent,³ and inspiration is a spiritual-divine power of truth, or of the ever

---

¹ Baur, *Dogm.-gesch.*, III : 423.
² Rudelbach, *Zeitsch. &c.*, 1840, *Zweit. Quart.*, 57.
³ *Von Freier Untersuchung des Canon*, 1 : 39.

forth-going word of God, which he, as it were, himself speaks within a man, and * * * in such a manner that he becomes sure that it is the instruction of God."¹

As matter of fact, Semler reduced inspiration from a human-subjective point of view to a mere devout frame of mind, and the 'testimonium Spiritus Sancti' to the advantage to be derived from the Scriptures for moral improvement and edification.

His practical application of these theories to the sacred canon and to theology in general needs no exposition here.

4. *Michaelis.*

Michaelis († 1791) wholly denied the orthodox interpretation of the 'testimonium Spiritus Sancti' and the 'fides divina' in connection with the doctrine of inspiration, conceding only that a 'good sound human understanding would find in the Scriptures themselves the proof of their divinity.' He frankly confessed in his 'Dogmatik' that, 'firmly as he was convinced of the truth of revelation, he had never in his life experienced the witness of the Holy Ghost, nor had he found in the entire Bible one word concerning it.'

5. *Griesbach.*

Griesbach († 1812) distinguished mediate natural inspiration, general religious enthusiasm, and providential guidance. The 'witness of the Spirit' in reference to the Scriptures was of less importance in his eyes than their usefulness for the moral improvement of man; '*authority*' gave place to *adaptedness to the end proposed.*² Some idea of his doctrinal attitude may be gained from the following passage: "The impartation of the Holy Ghost on the day of Pentecost qualified the disciples for the apostolic calling, and therefore for the composition of the writings necessarily connected with it. For extraordinary occasions there was bestowed a new, wonderful enduement of the Holy Spirit, but in addition, the natural mental activities of the sacred writers were preserved by Providence from *serious* error. How far the individual constituent parts of the sacred Scriptures have arisen from the one and the other source, cannot be distinguished, and

---

¹ Id., 46.

² Beck, *Dogm.-gesch.*, 121.

is not distinguished by the apostles themselves. Therefore the biblical idea of inspiration is the theocratic 'in-spiriting' of the *men*, not of the *writings*, for they were not 'in-spirited' to write.

6. Henke.

Henke († 1809) gave full and free expression to the rationalistic view, when he said that the sacred writers were moved to literary composition, and actually entered upon the work, from the desire of being serviceable to others, and from the opportunity thus presented; that they made choice of material according to the peculiar necessities of time and place, drew the facts themselves from the abundant resources of their own knowledge, the arrangement and embellishment of the same from their individual natural endowments, and the words from the habit and manner of speaking customary to each one.[1]

Every element which enters into the composition of the Scriptures is here referred to merely natural motives and causes.[2]

7. Herder.

Herder († 1803) is most conveniently and correctly mentioned here, both as a rationalist (though not of the school of Semler), and as a forerunner of Schleiermacher.

He sought to do away with what he viewed as the old materialistic idea of an inspired writing. As humanity, in the genuine sense, was to him the highest thing, so, said he, in order to humanize the Bible, which is the most human of all books, it must be read in a thoroughly human way. Inspiration, according to the orthodox interpretation, he characterizes as *nonsense*. A low habit of thinking in the dark ages liked to conceive of one who was moved by the divine Spirit, as an organ pipe through which the wind blows,—an empty machine from which all thoughts of its own are far removed. Cabbalistic ideas first gave birth to the conception of a sacred writing as a connected whole. These ideas were then propagated by the Alexandrian philosophy, and entered into Christianity. In the conflict with heretics, an appeal was made to an *in-spired Word*, and with the increase of ignorance, the lordship of *in-spiration* was founded, upon which finally Scholasticism set it seal. The word of God is nothing

---

[1] *Lineam., Instit. Fidis Christ.*, p. 39.
[2] Baur, *Dogm.-gesch.*, III: 427.

else than light—insight; among the Hebrews spirit and word were one. The Spirit which Christ promised to his followers was only his doctrine, his memory, his illuminated likeness.[1]

II. More Evangelical.

1. *Stapfer.*

This divine, theological professor at Berne († 1775) says: "We must distinguish between those parts of the sacred Scriptures which were written by the *immediate inspiration* of the Holy Ghost, and those which have been consigned to writing by his *direction* only. To the former class belong the peculiar discoveries of revelation respecting the way of salvation, predictions, etc. To the latter class belong truths already known from natural religion."

He adds, however: "Nor was any error permitted to creep in with regard even to the minutest fact or circumstance. All alike comes to us through inspiration, and is of equal precision, whether it be by revelation, observation, or reasoning; if we follow the latter, there can be no error in our conclusions, except by not properly applying the laws of interpretation."

III. Swedenborg.

Swedenborg's († 1772) doctrine of inspiration is unique and obscure. An adequate conception of it is to be gained only from the study of his writings, or at least from a detailed exposition of his views by one of his initiated disciples. The reader is referred, among other sources of information, to an article by Rev. Chauncey Giles, in the *North American Review*, October, 1878, pp. 314–319. Some of the following statements are taken from that paper.

With Swedenborg, the Scriptures and the word of God are identical, and are divine truth itself. "If the Word were not true," he says, "we could know nothing of God, of heaven or of hell, of life after death, and still less of the Lord." He held that man has no innate knowledge, but must *learn* everything he knows in every sphere. Revelation, therefore, is absolutely indispensable to teach him of beings and worlds that may exist beyond the realm of the senses.

---

[1] *Vom Geist des Christ., Werke zur Theol.*, XII: 235-6. Baur, III: 441.

It is to be noted that Swedenborg applies the term 'word of God,' not to our canonical books, but to another Scripture antedating and superior to ours. He calls it the 'Scripture of angels.' He advances also to another identification. As the Scripture is the 'word of God,' so the 'word of God' is the Lord himself. As God descended in order to become veritable man in the Son, so also does the Word—the divine proceeding from the Lord—that is, the Lord himself, descend through three stages to man. These stages are the celestial, the spiritual, and the natural.

In regard to those of the commonly received Scriptures which he admitted as canonical, he seems to have taught *degrees* of inspiration, for he distinguished the immediate utterances of God himself from those made by angels in his behalf. "The books spoken by the Lord, by the mouths of the prophets, were the five books of Moses, Joshua, Judges, First and Second Samuel, First and Second Kings, the Psalms, and all the Prophets from Isaiah to Malachi, the four Gospels and the Revelation." "The other books of the so-called canon are good and useful, and possess about the same kind and amount of inspiration generally accorded to the whole Bible, but they do not contain a connected spiritual meaning, and they are not therefore the word of the Lord, and they do not claim to be."[1]

All the sacred books alike stand in imperative need of a new revelation—that of Swedenborg—to render them intelligible.

Inspiration itself is the divine choice and use of natural forms for the expression of spiritual and eternal truth. Under the supernatural influence, speech and record alike become the faithful reflection of the Higher and Supreme Will.

With reference to the *extent* of inspiration, Swedenborg would seem to have accepted the verbal theory. At all events, he held single words of Scripture to be of so great importance as to fear, from the loss of the smallest of them, great peril to the whole connection of a passage. He appeals to the counting of the letters by the Massoretes as an arrangement of divine Providence for the preservation of the Scriptures from injury.[2]

The same verbal theory is suggested by his view that absolutely everything in Scripture is significant. Even the numbers and

---

[1] *N. A. Review*, October, 1878, 316.
[2] Baur, *Dogm.-gesch.*, III: 442.

the proper names have a spiritual meaning. Oftentimes the Scripture authors understood their own utterances only in their natural import, but this is of no importance. "The essential thing is that every word spoken should be the natural exponent of a divine truth, and that the Lord always provided for. There is not a word in the wildest vision of the prophets, in the driest genealogy, in the most natural precept, which does not embody a divine truth."[1]

IV. Opinion in England.

The indirect effect of Spinoza's thought, and the more direct influence of English divines above referred to, were seen in the loose ideas concerning inspiration prevalent both among churchmen and dissenters of England during the last century. The tendency was now, as it had been to some extent before, to limit the supernatural influence of the Holy Spirit upon the sacred writers to the religious element of the communications, and exclude it from all extraneous to that province. Among the opinions which diverged more or less from the standards of strict orthodoxy were those of—

1. *Whitby*.

The views of Whitby († 1726) upon inspiration may be arranged under two heads:

a. Nature.

As to its nature, it consists in such an impression by the Holy Ghost on the brain of a Scripture writer as to impart a clear idea of that which he wishes to communicate. Certainty is always given that the message is from God.[2]

b. Extent.

Two kinds or degrees of inspiration are distinguished:

That of *suggestion*, involving the communication of truth before unknown. This was exemplified primarily in the case of the prophets, though the apostles also, especially John, in writing the Apocalypse, gave evidence of the working of the same power.

That of *direction*. This implied such a divine superintendence

---

[1] *N. A. Review, October*, 1878, p. 318.

[2] *Preface to Comm. on N. T. Dissert. on Divine Authority of Scripture.*

as secured the sacred writers against all error, but presupposed that the general substance of the message was previously known by natural means — reason or education, or antecedent revelation.

Whitby would nowhere admit slips of memory on the part of the apostles, nor would he concede that they determined practical questions on grounds of human expediency, apart from the direction of the Holy Spirit.

He contended for such a kind and degree of inspiration as secured perfect certainty as to the truth written, but not for the theory of verbal, mechanical dictation.

2. *Samuel Clarke.*

Dr. Clarke († 1729) insisted upon a careful observance of the distinction between prophetic writings on the one hand, and historical and moral compositions on the other. He says that 'in the prophetic books, where the subject-matter was entirely new to the prophet himself, and very often perhaps not understood by him, it is very plain that inspiration means that the whole was dictated to the inspired writers, either in a vision, or by an angel, or otherwise, according as it pleased God to reveal himself at divers times and in diverse manners. But in the historical and moral books of Scripture, wherein the writers had themselves perfect knowledge of the facts recorded and of the doctrine taught, it was abundantly sufficient that they had such assistance of the Holy Spirit guiding them into *all* truth, as enabled them to express their own thoughts in their own words, with an effectual security that they should not err in the manner of delivering the doctrine which they were commanded to teach.[1]

3. *Calamy.*

Ed. Calamy († 1732) held that the divine assistance given to the sacred writers extended both to the formation of their conceptions and the framing of their writings; and that the assistance was of such sort as to prevent the insertion of anything false, or the omission of any necessary truth. The Spirit immediately suggested and dictated such things as were matters of pure revelation, and illuminated their minds in the several doctrinal and practical truths they delivered in writing.

---

[1] Works, vol. II: 86.

The Holy Ghost used the sacred penmen as reasonable creatures, and made use of their judgments, memories and affections, but they acted under his guidance in the whole of their work.

Natural difference of style and language, the Spirit did not obliterate but permitted in the writings drawn up under his conduct, save in some places where he thought fit to interfere in some particular strains of majesty and authority.

Inspiration did not imply immediate revelation. One is properly said to be inspired, if under such conduct of the divine Spirit as secures him from mistake and error.[1]

4. *Doddridge.*

Doddridge (†1751) distinguished different kinds or degrees of inspiration, after the manner of Whitby.

a. Inspiration of Superintendence.

This implies such a direction of the mind of a human writer of the Scriptures, that he is made more secure from error than he could have been by the mere use of his natural faculties. Complete freedom from error in declaring doctrines and stating facts implies plenary or full inspiration. Here many things may be known and recorded by the employment of the writer's unaided powers. The absolute truth of contents, both as to fact and doctrine, implies full inspiration, though the words, phrases, and manner be left to the human author, and imperfection of style and method be the result. In a book intended to teach truth for practical ends, such defects furnish no warrant for rejecting its authority. The New Testament was written under this inspiration.[2]

b. Inspiration of Elevation.

Where this occurs, such elevation of human powers is implied as to make the resulting productions more sublime, noble and pathetic than they could be as the result of merely natural genius. A part of the Bible was written under this inspiration. God only can draw the line here between the natural and the super-

---

[1] *Inspiration of the Old and New Testaments*, pp. 30 ff.
[2] *Dissertation on Inspiration.* Works, vol. II: 194.

natural. Such inspiration may possibly have existed in the case of some heathen writers.

c. Inspiration of Suggestion.

This is the highest kind, and exists when God speaks directly to the mind, communicating what it could not otherwise know, dictating every word, making the human author a mere auditor or secretary of the divine. The Apocalypse and some other parts of the New Testament were written under this influence.[1]

5. *Bishop Warburton.*

This prelate († 1779) calls the verbal dictation theory of inspiration 'a spurious opinion, begotten in the *Jewish* church by superstition, and nursed up by mistaken piety in the *Christian*, which hath almost passed into an article of faith.'[2] This shows incidentally the strength and prevalence of orthodox views in England during his day.

After stating the objections to the strict theory, and, as he thinks, proving their validity, he sets forth his own idea of inspiration somewhat as follows: 'The Holy Spirit so directed the pens of the writers that no considerable error should fall from them. He enlightened their minds with his immediate influence in all such matters as were necessary for the instruction of the church, but was content to preserve them by the more ordinary means of providence from any mistakes of consequence concerning those things which they had learned by the common way of information. In short, he watched over them incessantly, but with so suspended a hand as permitted the use, and left them to the guidance of their own faculties while they kept clear of error.'[3]

He anticipates and refutes the objection that this 'partial inspiration,' so called, does not enable us to distinguish the parts of Scripture which were written under the influence of the Spirit, and those which were the product of human knowledge only. "What matters this?" he says. "All we need to be assured of is that every sentence of Scripture which but remotely concerns

---

[1] *Dissertation on Inspiration.*

[2] Works, vol. VIII. *Doctrine of Grace,* 273.

[3] *Doct. of Grace,* pp. 275, 276.

either faith or practice, is infallibly true.[1] It is no matter how truth comes to us, if only we have it fully and certainly."

He thinks the partial theory important from an apologetic point of view, 'to free the infallible word of Scripture from all those embarassing circumstances which have been so artfully and disingenuously thrown out to its discredit.'[2]

6. *Middleton.*

Dr. C. Middleton († 1750), though a noted divine and scholar of the Church of England, has often been regarded as a disbeliever in the fundamental truths of Christianity. Not only did his views diverge from those even of the English latitudinarians hitherto considered, but his whole spirit and character were so different that, with his disciple Wakefield, he deserves a place by himself at the end of the list.

His aim seems to have been to eradicate as far as possible the supernatural element from the Scriptures, and to subvert by any and every possible method the received view of their infallible inspiration. He says bitterly that the orthodox doctrine on this subject is 'a clog and incumbrance to Christianity with all rational and thinking men,' and 'has no other foundation but in the mistaken sense of certain texts suggested by the prejudice of pious men.'[3] He grounds these statements partly on the so-called evidence of fact, saying that 'everyone may see apparent marks of human frailty in the Scriptures, not only in style and language, but sometimes also in matter.'

The evangelists make not the least pretensions to infallibility, and the apostles on some occasions distinctly disclaim it. 'Paul was sometimes destitute of divine assistance in explaining particular doctrines; and contradictions exist in the gospels which are incapable of reconciliation.[4] Two examples of his style of criticism may illustrate his spirit and method:

"Matthew either wilfully suppressed or negligently omitted three successive descents from father to son in the first chapter of his gospel.[5]

---

[1] *Doct. of Grace*, p. 277.
[2] Id., 279.
[3] Works, vol. II: 19, 20.
[4] *Reflections on the Variations found in the Four Evangelists.*
[5] Works, vol. II: 24.

With reference to the protevangelic promise, "men who inquire into things will meet with many absurdities which reason must wink at, and many incredibilities which faith must digest, before they can admit the authority of this prophecy upon the evidence of this historical narration."[1]

7. *Wakefield.*

Gilbert Wakefield († 1801) published (1781) an 'Essay on Inspiration,' which is thus summed up by Mr. Leslie Stephen[2]: "He argued that the inspiration of the gospel was 'unnecessary because strength of judgment, adequate information and unbiased affection are sufficient guarantees for historical accuracy.' It was 'inexpedient and improbable' because a complete consistency would have led to suspicions of complicity.

"It was disclaimed by the writers themselves, and cases of absolute contradiction could be produced. Christ wished to show the efficacy of truth operating without supernatural advantages."

Mr. Stephen sets down the production as little more than an imitation of the older attack of Middleton.

I. THE DOCTRINE OF INSPIRATION IN THE NINETEENTH CENTURY.

We have already passed the dividing line which separates the present century from the past, and here perhaps a purely historical survey should stop. Yet surely the questions concerning inspiration are living ones, and possess an interest and importance other than that which is strictly historical. Some enthusiasts call them the 'burning, blazing' questions of the day and hour. We may at least be justified in presenting a sketch of the opinions of some leading and representative writers.

I. German Rationalists.

1. *Wegscheider.*

Wegscheider († 1849) held that the power by which the Scripture writers were enabled to fulfil their task differed in no essential

---

[1] *Works*, Vol. III: 183.
[2] *Hist. of Eng. Thought in the Eighteenth Century*, Vol. II: 142-3.

respect from that possessed in common by all men as a gift from the Almighty, and manifested in the ordinary exercise of the moral and rational nature. He therefore made the essence of inspiration to consist simply in the fact that the sacred writers, in the spirit of piety, referred to God their good thoughts and ideas, and recorded them under divine guidance and assistance.[1]

2. *De Wette.*

This theologian († 1849) says: "The biblical doctrine of inspiration does not imply the superstitious notion of an influence of the Holy Ghost upon the sacred writers, abrogating the laws of nature, nor the exaggerated extension of inspiration to all things and everything in the Scriptures, nor yet the admission of their unconditional and unlimited infallibility.

"The essential idea is rather the religious sense of the divine working, or of the Holy Spirit, in the sacred writers, and this indeed solely in regard to their belief and elevation of soul, not in regard to their formation of ideas. It bore relation to historic truth, only in so far as its knowledge was dependent upon a holy love of truth."[2]

Baur criticises this as the familiar phraseology with which rationalism seeks to conceal the shallowness of its views.[3]

II. Schleiermacher.

Schleiermacher († 1834) gave up the old ecclesiastical theory of inspiration, and advocated views which formed on the whole its direct antithesis. These views, utterly unsound from the standpoint of orthodoxy, were yet thought to mark essential progress in the history of the doctrine.

Schleiermacher taught:

1. That the Spirit by which the Scriptures are inspired is not the personal Holy Ghost, but rather the 'genius' of Christianity individualizing itself in the sacred writers, and related to them as the general to the particular. This theologian promptly dismisses every question as to the more exact relation of this Holy Ghost to the Third Person of the Trinity.

---

[1] *Institutiones*, § 44.

[2] *Dogmatik der Luth. Kirch.*, p. 41.

[3] *Dogm.-gesch.*, III: 428.

2. The idea of inspiration is to be properly understood only from the history in which it appears. This inseparable connection of the inspiration-idea and a definite history, Schleiermacher maintains, and makes his point of departure. Cremer remarks: "Whether his conception is sufficiently broad and attaches to actual history, or merely to the theory of the same, is another matter."[1]

3. Inspiration was not a transient state, but a permanent attribute of the apostles—a part of their collective official activity. It was monstrous, he held, to maintain (for the purpose of giving special prominence to the inspiration of the Scriptures) that the apostles were less animated and moved by the Holy Ghost in other parts of their official work than in the act of writing.[2] Special apostolic inspiration is nothing appertaining exclusively to the New Testament books: these only participate in it, and inspiration in this narrower sense, as it is conditioned by the purity and completeness of the apostolic apprehension of Christianity, so it extends to all the official apostolic activity proceeding therefrom.[3]

4. The New Testament, on the other hand (while strictly supernatural neither in origin nor contents), is yet the most original and the purest expression of the new life flowing from Christ. No subsequent writings can be compared with those whose authors stood under the purifying influence of his living memory. To all later works they must possess, in some sense, a normative significance and relation.

5. So far as the Old Testament is concerned, Schleiermacher taught that it proceeded not from the 'genius' (gemein-geist) of Christianity, but from the narrow national spirit of Judaism. Belief in its special inspiration, or in the fact of a revelation made to the Jewish people, he regarded as inconsistent with the advanced stage of information respecting Jewish history. Faith in the revelation of God in Christ, he declared, was in no way dependent upon the acceptance of the Jewish canon.[4] He explained the admission of the Old Testament books to a place in

---

[1] Herzog, *Art. Inspiration*, 757.
[2] Baur, *Dogm. gesch.*, III: 429.
[3] Id. ib.
[4] Id., III: 444.

the Christian canon, partly from the appeals made to them by New Testament writers, and partly from the historical connection between Christian worship and the Jewish synagogue.¹

Rationalistic as these views of Schleiermacher clearly were, it is nevertheless true that the general influence, both of the man himself and of his doctrinal system, was opposed to rationalism, and in favor of positive faith in a positive revelation.

III. Supernaturalism.

This was a product of the transition period, and, while maintaining old forms of expression, departed essentially from the old orthodox Lutheran faith. The older divines had based their theory of inspiration upon the inner necessity of the thing; the supernaturalists founded theirs on the promise of Christ to bestow his Spirit on the apostles. The historical certainty of inspiration, then, rested upon the authority and trustworthiness of Jesus as an immediate divine teacher.² 'Supernaturalism' found the supernatural element in revelation, not in the *form* but in the *contents* of the sacred writings. Upon *revelation* it laid chief stress, and viewed the apostles as the chief witnesses thereto.³ To this school the trustworthiness of the Scriptures was of supreme importance, rather than their divine origin and authority. It was believed that in the written records, the assistance of the Spirit was enjoyed to such a degree as to preserve the authors from error in matters of faith. In regard to non-essentials they were left to the exercise of their own faculties, and of course were fallible.

1. *Twesten.*

This divine was one of the supernaturalists attaching himself to the school of Schleiermacher. Like Nitzsch, he professed not to deviate essentially from the definitions of the older theologians, but rather to accept them. None the less does he confess a multitude of weaknesses in the old theory, and therefore make the more desperate effort to save his orthodoxy, and at the same time preserve his allegiance to his master. He actually succeeded, like other divines of this class, in wavering between the two.⁴

---

¹ Beck, *Dogm.-gesch.*, 123.
² Baur, *Dogm.-gesch.*, III: 428.
³ Kahnis, *Luther. Dogm.*, 288.
⁴ Baur, *Dogm.-gesch.*, III: 430.

2. *Elwert.*

'It was reserved for Elwert († 1865) to develop most thoroughly the theory of inspiration based upon principles laid down by Schleiermacher. This view supposes the apostles to have been inspired, only in so far as the Spirit works in them a faith by which they appropriated to themselves the revelation of Christ, and so far as from this, by means of faith, in the natural way of reflection, their religious ideas and conceptions found development.'[1]

The differences between this later and the earlier idea of inspiration, are thus summed up.[2]

a. "The sacred writers in the composition of their works were by no means in a purely passive condition; they rather made use of their natural powers and capacities, and impressed upon their productions unmistakably the stamp of their own individuality.

b. "The possession of the Holy Ghost in the case of the apostles was generically one with the participation of others in the same gift; but, agreeably to the end which was to be accomplished through them, and conformably to their relation to the original revelation in Christ, it was in their case pre-eminent in degree.

c. "The influence of the Holy Ghost upon them was not a suggestion of elaborated ideas and knowledges. The Spirit rather wrought in them the faith which was the mediating element between their religious conceptions and the revelation of Christ.

d. "The operation of the Holy Ghost is to be referred, not so much to individual matters as to the whole manner of thinking and feeling on the part of the apostles, within whom he dwelt as a permanent principle. The older theory was *right* in so far as it admitted his activity in every single part: in the resolution to write, in the formation of the thoughts and words, and in selection and arrangement. But it was *wrong* in this, that it admitted that relation of the divine activity at all points, equally and immediately.

e. "The idea of an unconditional infallibility of the apostolic writings is to be abandoned. Infallible they were, in so far as this, that they, and indeed they alone, lead the Christian soul to

---

[1] Baur, *Dogm.-gesch.*, III: 430.
[2] Id. ib.

life in Christ, and transmit the fundamental truths in a perfectly trustworthy way. In other respects infallibility cannot be proved.

f. "The *form* belongs to the individuality of the apostles, and the influences they derived from their age. Each age has to conceive Christian doctrine in the form peculiar to it, and to mould it into system. If this form is penetrated with the spirit of Christianity, then all the manifoldness of the same is unattended with danger. For it is the way of the Spirit to exhibit itself in manifold form. Just because it is the Spirit of Eternal Revelation, it cannot, Christ excepted, express itself fully and completely in any finite spirit." [1]

IV. More General Evangelical.

This term is intended merely as a designation of the general views and sympathies of the writers whose names appear under it, without attempting to define more exactly their precise theological position.

1. *Neander.*

This divine († 1850), declared his conviction that it was necessary to distinguish what is *divine* from what is *human* in the gospel record. "I am sure," he says, "that the fall of the old form of the doctrine of inspiration, and indeed of many other doctrinal prejudices, will not only not involve the fall of the essence of the gospel, but will cause it no detriment whatever. Nay, I believe it will be more clearly and accurately understood, and men will be better prepared to fight with and conquer that inrushing infidelity, against which the weapons of the old dogmatism must be powerless in any land, and that from such a struggle a new theology, purified and renovated in the spirit of the gospel, must arise." [2]

Neander's own view of inspiration may be gathered from the following passage: "If we find, on close inquiry, that the historical statements of the evangelists are somewhat obscured by subjective influences, our estimate of their veracity need in no wise be affected thereby. Such a result would not conflict in the least with the only tenable idea of inspiration. The organs which the Holy Ghost illuminated and inspired to convey his

---

[1] Baur, *Dogm.-gesch*, III, 431.
[2] *Life of Christ*, Pref. p. xi.

truth to men, retained their individual peculiarites, and remained within the sphere of the psychological laws of our being. Besides, inspiration, both in its nature and its object, refers only to man's religious interests, and to points connected with it."[1]

2. *Stier.*

Stier († 1862) attempted to vindicate the old Lutheran doctrine of verbal inspiration, but could not avoid important critical concessions.

His theory was in some respects peculiar. He maintained that the Scriptures give us the thoughts, not of its individual authors, but of the Spirit, speaking through them. Inspiration applies not to the words but to *the Word.* "We possess what Christ spoke, not indeed the very words themselves, literally understood, but as indicated through the testimony of the Evangelists, and elevated into the Spirit."

The Scripture is infallible so far as general tenor is concerned, though there may be inaccuracies in minor matters. Being firm in the orthodox faith that the Holy Spirit is the primary author of Scripture, Stier did not trouble himself about the canonicity of the human authors. In his own development of the doctrine of inspiration, he exhibited an evangelical mystic tendency.

3. *Philippi.*

The general sympathies of Philippi were with the conservative and strict construction of our doctrine. Yet he comprehends inspiration under the more general idea of 'illumination,' i. e., the enlightening influence of the divine Spirit upon the church, from which, however, he is careful to distinguish it in various ways.[2] He defines inspiration as 'that act of the Spirit of God upon the human spirit, by means of which the latter becomes, as it were the object of revelation, and is enabled to receive it pure and unsullied;' or, 'that contact of the human spirit with the Spirit of God through which the revelation of the latter, in its pure and undistorted forms, becomes the possession of the former.'[3]

He distinguishes three *degrees* of inspiration—the legal, the prophetic, and the apostolic, each higher, more complete, and

---
[1] *Life of Christ*, p. 47.
[2] *Kirchl. Glaubensl.*, 1: 207-21.
[3] Id., 1: 222-3.

perfect than the other.¹ The last or apostolic stage is substantially coincident with revelation, the difference between the two being ideal rather than actual.

4. *Rothe.*

Rothe († 1867) maintained with steadfast determination the revealed character of Christianity. He did indeed abandon the old theory of inspiration, but only to undertake its scientific reconstruction on what seemed to him more sure foundations.²

To him the Bible is not the word of God, in the sense of an immediate communication of religious doctrine.³ It is not revelation itself, but rather its record, in the purest and fullest meaning of the term. It is simply the overflow of the fulness of the divine life of its authors. The Bible is not inspired, in the old dogmatic sense of the word, for inspiration does not relate to literary activity. It is not a religious text-book, but rather a historical record, which, as a constituent part of revelation,⁴ must be penetrated and surrounded by the peculiar atmosphere of the same, i. e., by the divine breath which it inhales. Nevertheless, from its historic character it must be content patiently to abide the free scientific investigations of historical criticism respecting the canon as a whole, and the canonicity of single parts; for the great revolution in religious knowledge which characterizes modern times finds the foundation and centre of Christianity, not in a book, but in a *person;* not in a doctrinal system, but in facts and deeds, i. e., in history.⁵

5. *Martensen.*

Martensen, bishop of Seeland, Denmark, occupies in general the position of Rothe, though modified by the influence of Schleiermacher. With reference to—

a. The Nature of Inspiration

he holds, in the first place, to an inseparable union between the miracle of the Incarnation and that of inspiration. Properly speaking, they are only the two sides—one objective and the other

---

¹ *Kirchl. Glaubensl.*, I: 223 ff.
² Kahnis, *Luther. Dogm.*, 287.
³ Rothe, *Zur Dogmatik* (1863); *Dritte Abhand.*, 155.
⁴ Id., 26, 129, 319.
⁵ Id. 317.

subjective—of the one fundamental miracle of the new creation, to which the Christian church traces its origin.¹

The miracle of inspiration took place on the day of Pentecost, and was the breaking forth of the Spirit of God within the spirit of man. The gift of tongues was essentially a state of ecstasy, but this did not constitute inspiration. It was only its accompaniment, and as it were a shell or husk, within which was contained, and out of which proceeded the clear and historical consciousness of revelation.²

Inspiration in the primitive age was not confined exclusively to the apostles, but (distinguishing degrees in the same) was bestowed upon them in its *fulness* for their official work as founders of the church.³ Their relation to the Spirit was not one of bondage, but rather of freedom; and in their case inspiration consisted in a progressive communication of the Spirit, going hand in hand with the progressive development both of consciousness and of freedom.⁴ Personality in the Scripture writers was therefore not lost, but preserved, intensified and elevated. It is to be noted also that not the individual, but the total apostolic consciousness can be taken as an adequate expression of the mind of the Spirit; and this was raised above temporal limitations and imperfections only in regard to the articles of fundamental truth.⁵

In the Holy Scriptures Martensen finds the ripened fruit of inspiration. He would emphasize both the *union* and the *distinction* of the divine and human elements contained therein.⁶ The formula of the former is, 'the Scripture *is* the word of God;' that of the latter, 'the Scriptures *contain* the word of God.' Each is true when properly defined and explained.

b. The Extent of Inspiration.

Martensen would not extend inspiration to every tittle and every point in the Bible.⁷ Something transient and casual exists in every book of the Old Testament, and also in the New. We cannot maintain the representative character of everything in the

---

[1] *Christian Dogmatics*, 19.
[2] Id., 338, 339.
[3] Id., 342.
[4] Id., 342.
[5] Id., 343, 402, 403.
[6] Id., 403.
[7] Id., ib.

New Testament as a pattern for our guidance: e. g. community of goods, combination of the agapæ with the Lord's supper, &c. Only the general practice of the church is exemplary for permanent guidance.'

He does not view possible or actual contradictions in chronological and historical details as harmful, unless of such a kind as to affect the *substance* of revelation, i. e. to distort our apprehension of Christ's person, or disturb the fundamental basis of revealed truth.[2]

6. *Hofman.*

This divine was inclined to a free construction of the doctrine of inspiration.[3] He regarded the limitation of the idea to Scripture as unwarranted and arbitrary, and would himself extend it to heathen writings and poets. He said that the doctrine of inspiration was nothing else than a 'conclusion-backward' (Rückschluss) from the *character* of the Scriptures to their *origin*. From this view also resulted the theory of its infallibility. He would not himself admit that the teaching of any single apostle was absolutely free from error; much less could any one portraiture of Christ adequately set forth the full glory of its subject. He did affirm, however, that the *collective* preaching of the apostles contained the conditions of an absolutely errorless apprehension of Christ. (Compare Martensen above.) The Bible, accordingly, is not wholly free from error, but it is the perfectly sufficient instrument for attaining an absolutely infallible knowledge of divine revelation, since it contains within itself the means of self-purification from the errors clinging to its individual parts: i. e. it contains the means of self-correction. This is its *actual* infallibility, and herein also lies its sufficiency.[4]

7. *Tholuck.*

This theologian in his 'Essay on the Doctrine of Inspiration' maintains:

a. That what is known as the old orthodox theory (i. e. the high Lutheran) is in reality modern, not dating back even to the Reformation.

---

[1] *Christian Dogmatics*, 405.
[2] Id., 404.
[3] *Schrift-beweis, passim.*
[4] Beck, *Dogm.-gesch.*, 127.

b. That it was developed as a means of furnishing to Protestantism a counter-infallibility to that claimed by Catholicism for œcumenical councils and the pope.

c. That in reality it has placed in the hands of rationalism a most formidable weapon of attack upon the church.

d. That the free conception of the doctrine, so far from being the fruit of modern rationalism, has had its advocates in every age of the church, and must perforce find recognition and acceptance as the result of careful and candid reflection upon the text of Scripture.[1]

The main part of the essay is an ardent polemic against the received doctrine of the absolute inspiration and infallibility of the Scriptures, evidence being drawn not only from the history of opinion, but also from the character and constitution of the sacred books themselves. He asserts the clear and certain existence of imperfections and errors in the Scriptures as we have them, but thinks that so long as these do not touch essential matters, i. e. the substance of revealed truth, they can do no damage to Christian faith, nor to the doctrine of inspiration properly conceived. The witness of the Spirit is certain to faith, and faith once become conscious of its own essential character, unhesitatingly leaves to science all that transcends this province.[2]

Tholuck's work thus appears to be mainly negative or destructive. He has, however, positive convictions of his own, and devotes the concluding part of the essay to a defence and proof of his position, that a divine and infallible inspiration, i. e. a direct and absolute witness of the Spirit, does relate to the *kernel* of Scripture, in other words, to its properly *revealed parts*, including everything that concerns the Christian doctrine of salvation.

8. *Düsterdieck*.

Düsterdieck published, a number of years since, a volume entitled "Apologetische Beiträge," mainly devoted to the question of inspiration in relation to the individuality of the sacred writers, and their real or supposed mistakes.

He believes that they did fall into errors, e. g., such as that of expecting Christ's near return, but holds that this did not in any measure detract from their authority.

---

[1] Baur, *Dogm.-gesch.*, III: 439.
[2] Tholuck, translated in *Noyes' Theol. Essays*, 105, 106.

"I believe," he says, "on the one hand, in a theory of inspiration which admits the possibility of errors, not only in historical and other external matters, but even in matter of doctrine. On the other hand, I reject every theory of the nature of the Scriptures, and the inspiration of its writers as *false* and *destructive*, which is incompatible with Paul's declaration in 1 Thess. ii: 13, "When ye received the word of God which ye heard of us, ye received it not as the word of men, but, as it is in truth, the word of God."

9. *Hengstenberg.*

The views of this theologian († 1869) upon inspiration seem in many respects like those of 'one born out of due time,' but really correspond with his reactionary ideas upon other matters. He occupied very nearly the position of Philo and of Justin Martyr, and the other old apologists.

He finds the source of inspiration in prophetic ecstasy, which necessarily involves the cessation of human agency and intelligent perception. The Hebrew seers were not merely passive instruments, but were actually rapt into a state of prophetic frenzy, raving like the Pythian priestess or the other heathen sibyls and soothsayers of antiquity. The other developments of Hengstenberg's theory can easily be imagined.

10. *Van Oosterzee.*

This representative of the evangelical Dutch school may be most conveniently mentioned here. He holds—

a. As to the *nature* of inspiration, that it was not an external, mechanical, blindly impelling force, but a heavenly influence inwardly exerted upon the writers, whereby they were guided and strengthened for self-activity.[1] It did not therefore prejudice, but rather enlarge, intensify and glorify their individuality. The Holy Spirit took possession of each man, and used him as, according to the nature of his sanctified personality, he really was.

Inspiration is not to be conceived as a mere momentary assistance granted to the sacred writers exclusively in and during the act of writing, but as the natural consequence of their being

---

[1] *Christian Dogmatics*, I: 200.

personally led by the Holy Ghost, who controlled their thinking and working, and in this way also their writing.¹

b. These men were in a special manner, but in *varying degrees*, the organs of the Holy Ghost.

c. Inspiration extended not only to great but to little things in Scripture, not only to the things taught, but to the words and the whole style of speech. This is argued from the indissoluble union of form and contents; and archaisms, solecisms and other peculiarities are not judged inconsistent with this view.²

d. Inspiration had its limits.

Van Oosterzee admits real contradictions in the Scriptures, and denies unlimited and infallible inspiration, except in regard to that which concerns God's saving truth.³

Our study of the doctrine of inspiration as held by the theologians of modern Germany cannot fail to impress us strongly with two facts: one, the strong reaction in religious minds against the destructive excesses of theological rationalism in the last century, with especial reference to our doctrine; and the other, the equally strong opposition to the rigid dogma as held and taught by the Protestant scholastics of the seventeenth century.

Whatever the varying standpoints of the German theology of the present age, all forms, with rare exceptions, agree in the common demand of a fuller recognition of the *human side* of the Scriptures. It generally admits in regard to the *nature* of inspiration, no genuine and fundamental distinction between the operation of the Holy Spirit upon the minds of the sacred writers, and upon common Christian believers. The difference is not one of kind, but only of degree.

As to *extent*, inspiration covers only what are technically called *essential truths*,—room is left for endless imperfections, both of form and of fact, provided the latter concern only minor details. Where the line shall be drawn between the 'minor' and the 'major,' is confessedly more difficult to determine.

The Bible *is* not, but *contains* the word of God. Not writings but men were inspired.

---

[1] *Christian Dogmatics*, I: 201.

[2] Id 203.

[3] Id. 202.

V. French Orthodoxy.

Modern French orthodoxy with reference to the doctrine of inspiration finds its chief representatives in Gasparin and Gaussen. Both have published treatises which have been translated into English.[1] Other writers have taken much more moderate views.

1. *Gaussen.*

This divine († 1863) taught the absolute inspiration and divinity of the Scriptures in every part—including form as well as substance, expression as well as matter. He says: "The word of God is God speaking in man, God speaking by man, God speaking as man, God speaking for man."

In regard to Paul's assertion that "all Scripture is given by inspiration of God, &c.," he remarks: "It admits of no restriction; it is the *whole Scripture*, all that is written ($\pi\tilde{\alpha}\sigma\alpha\ \gamma\rho\alpha\phi\acute{\eta}$)—that is to say, the thoughts that have already put on the clothing of language. It admits of no restriction; all Scripture is so far a work of God that it is represented as given to us by the breath of God, in the same manner as the word of a man is given by the breath of his mouth. The prophet is the mouth of the Most High."[2] Again: "The entire Bible is not only named the 'Word of God' ($\dot{o}\ \lambda\acute{o}\gamma o\varsigma\ \tau o\tilde{v}\ \vartheta\varepsilon o\tilde{v}$), it is called without distinction, the 'Oracles of God' ($\tau\grave{\alpha}\ \lambda\acute{o}\gamma\iota\alpha\ \tau o\tilde{v}\ \vartheta\varepsilon o\tilde{v}$). Who does not know what the oracles were in the opinion of the ancients? Was there then a single word which could express more absolutely a complete and verbal inspiration?"[3]

Gaussen professes to admit, and tries to illustrate the preservation of the individuality of the sacred writers when under the influence of inspiration. He repudiates all notion of the state of ecstasy, and maintains their self-control. He yet refers all differences in biblical accounts of the same transaction, and indeed all the human as well as the divine phenomena, to the Holy Ghost as their author. Immediate and universal divine efficiency, and coexistent human freedom and individuality, he affirms. To reconcile or explain the two, he finds of course a very different matter.

---

[1] Gasparin, "*Plenary Inspiration*," translated by *Montgomery.*
Gaussen, "*Theopneustic*," 1842. *Eng. trans.* by *Kirk*, 1846.
[2] Gaussen, p. 345.
[3] Id., p. 355.

2. *Meylan.*

M. Auguste Meylan, a Swiss Protestant pastor, published in 1877 a treatise on the Canonicity and Inspiration of the Scriptures. His positions are, for a continental divine, on the whole decidedly conservative. He defines inspiration as "that action of God upon the sacred writers, which put them in a condition to receive the revelation in its integrity, and transmit it to us without alteration."[1]

He disavows all sympathy with dictation theories, and allows a human factor in the composition of the Scriptures. He admits progress in the course of divine revelation, and degrees in inspiration, varying according to the requirements and circumstances of the case. He even concedes contradictions in matters of minor detail among the sacred narratives, but repudiates the consequences of such concessions.

The author is unable to bring himself to the admission of the distinctions, so generally recognized by continental writers upon inspiration, between that element in the Bible which stands in relation to human salvation, and that which has no connection with it. Once, however, he seems to approximate the idea, (p. 188.)

M. Meylan admits a difference of *kind*, and not merely of *degree* between apostolic authors and Christian writers in general, thus arraying himself against the the rationalists, and allying himself with pronounced advocates of evangelical orthodox opinions.

3. *Godet.*

Dr. Godet, professor at Neuchatel, approving in general the definition of inspiration given by Meylan, yet declares his conviction that the true light can be shed upon the circle of questions relating thereto (perhaps the most difficult in all sacred science), only by a clear and frank admission of the distinction between the Bible and the word of God. The Bible includes more than the immediate revelation of God. It *contains* the word of God, but is not *identical with* it. Nothing can be more delicate than the problems which grow out of this distinction, but the time has come for the church to rise to the recognition of this important fact.[2]

---

[1] Revue Chretienne, 1878, p. 57.
[2] Id., ib.

French rationalism, in the persons of Edmund Scherer, Colani and other writers in the "Revue de Theologie," has asserted German freedom of investigation.

VI. Opinion in England.

We have seen that the evangelic orthodoxy of Germany has not yet recovered from the blighting effects of the rationalistic reaction of the eighteenth century against the dogmatic exaggerations and absurdities of the seventeenth. It is but fair then to notice that in Great Britain and America a counter-revolution set in against previously prevailing latitudinarianism, in favor of higher, stricter and more churchly views concerning the divine origin and character of the Holy Scriptures. The doctrine of the plenary inspiration and infallible authority of the Bible has had during the present century a long line of champions, all of whom with pious intent, and not a few with learning and acuteness, have defended what was to them the cause of truth, and foundation of the 'faith once delivered.' The reader will at once recall the names of many distinguished writers, whose works are in every reference library, and some of them the companion of every pastor in his study.

To attempt to sketch these views, set forth often in extended monographs, would be impossible and useless, especially as this sketch is not intended for the defense of imperilled orthodoxy. The historic interest may be best served by noting chiefly the *deviations* from generally received opinions, among writers and scholars of varying schools of thought.

1. *Paley.*

This divine († 1805) says: "The doctrines came to the apostles by revelation. They were wont to illustrate, support and enforce them by such analogies, arguments and considerations as their own thoughts suggested.

"The doctrine must be received, but it is not necessary, in order to defend Christianity, to maintain the propriety of every comparison, or the validity of every argument which an apostle has brought into the discussion."[1]

---

[1] *Evidences of Christianity*, Pt. III: ch. 2.

2. *Priestly.*

Dr. Priestly († 1808) holds us bound to consider the great truths uttered by the apostles as from God—divine, and worthy of the highest regard. He judges us not bound, however, to accord like faith to the minutiæ of what they mention, nor to their arguments and reasonings either from facts or revealed doctrines.

3. *Heber.*

Bishop Heber († 1826) declares[1] that 'mistakes in points where inspiration does not properly apply, can by no means derogate from the inspired character of a work, in those respects where inspiration is either needed or promised.' He also says that 'circumstances which, whether true or false, have no positive bearing on the doctrine or character of Christ, may belong indeed to his history, but are no essential parts of the gospel.' The bishop insists that the *words of Christ* are reported by the evangelists with supernatural and infallible authority.

4. *Parry.*

Wm. Parry († 1818) endeavored to prove that there was no necessity for inspiration or immediate divine suggestion of what the apostles knew already, either from the discourses of Christ or their own observation. The Holy Spirit taught them all things respecting Christianity, of which they were not previously in possession—the whole of that *religious truth* which it was necessary for them to teach, or for men to know. Since he preserved them from all error in what they taught and recorded, the same result is secured as though he had dictated every syllable of their writings. If they had been mere machines under his direction, they could in no case have given to men more than a *perfect rule* as to all religious opinions and duties, all matters of faith and practice. But such a perfect rule we have in the New Testament, if we consider the writers as under the Spirit's infallible guidance in all the religious sentiments they express, whether he suggested the very words in which they are written or not.[2]

---

[1] *Bampton Lectures* (1815), pp. 301-2.
[2] *Inquiry into the Nature and Extent of the Inspiration of the Apostles*, &c.

5. *Coleridge.*

It was Coleridge († 1834), perhaps, more than any one else, who really domesticated in England, and put in permanent circulation there, views on the subject of inspiration hitherto current chiefly in Germany, and based rather upon profound acquaintance with German metaphysical philosophy, than with the genuine science of Christian theology. The theory propounded in his 'Confessions of an Inquiring Spirit'[1] is known sometimes as the '*subjective*,' and again as one form of the '*partial*' theory. Really it is both subjective and partial.

a. He distinguishes carefully *immediate divine revelation*, contained in the Law and the Prophets (and of course absolutely infallible), from *inspiration*, or the actuation and assistance of the Holy Spirit vouchsafed to the authors of other parts of Scripture. The latter is only the 'highest degree of that grace and communion of the Spirit, which the church under all circumstances, and every regenerate member of the church, is permitted to hope and instructed to pray for.' In other words, supernatural inspiration, in the proper sense of the term, belongs only to the Law and the Prophets.

b. Consistently with his view, Coleridge admits errors and discrepancies in those matters which 'stand in no necessary connection with the known and especial ends and purposes of the Scriptures.'

c. He bases his belief in the divinity of the Scriptures, chiefly upon the testimony of inward personal experience. 'Whatever *finds* me, bears witness for itself that it has proceeded from a Holy Spirit.'

Some younger friends and followers of Coleridge abandoned his careful distinction between revelation and inspiration, wholly displaced the supernatural element from the Bible, and ascribed to it only such inspiration as is common to all believers.

6. *Arnold.*

One of the pupils of Thos. Arnold († 1842) asserts that he had no accurate, precise, and sharply defined view of inspiration.[2]

---

[1] *Works*, Vol. V: 569 ff.
[2] B. Price, in Stanley's *Life of Arnold*, 197.

This may be true, and yet it may not be difficult to form reasonably distinct impressions as to his general ideas. According to the same authority, he found and acknowledged in the Bible an oracle from God, a positive and supernatural revelation made to man, an immediate inspiration of the Spirit.'

Many utterances on the subject of inspiration are found in his 'Sermons on the Christian Life: Its Course, Hindrances and Helps.' Thus he says: "Paul had the Spirit of God so abundantly that no human being ever enjoyed a larger share," and asks, "Are not his writings most truly to be called inspired? Can any reasonable mind doubt that to refuse to believe his testimony is really to disbelieve God?"²

While Arnold holds, however, that the Scriptures are divinely framed and superintended, he would not have his faith depend on the accuracy of a date or a minute historical particular.³ He calls it an unwarranted interpretation of the term 'inspiration,' to believe that it is equivalent to a communication of divine perfections.⁴ In whatever points errors may be discernible in Scripture, either it does not concern what God has done for us, or what we are to do for him; or, if it seems to do so, God has made some provision for the case, to remove what it might otherwise have had of difficulty.

The following utterances will convey some idea of his views as to the *extent* of the divine influence upon the minds of the sacred writers: "Inspiration does not raise a man above his own time, or make him, even in respect to that which he utters when inspired, perfect in wisdom and goodness; but it so overrules his language that it shall contain a meaning more than his own mind was conscious of, and thus give to it a character of divinity and a power of perpetual application."⁵

7. *Robertson.*

The views of F. W. Robertson († 1853), are best disclosed in two letters, Nos. cxxxix and cxl of his "Life and Letters."⁶

---

¹ Stanley, *Life of Arnold*, 197.
² *Sermons*, p. 400.
³ Id. 398.
⁴ Id. 399.
⁵ *Sermon on Interpretation of Scripture*, 141, Eng. Ed.
⁶ Harper's Edition, pp. 306-7.

"The prophetic power, in which, I suppose, is chiefly exhibited that which we mean by inspiration, depends almost entirely on moral greatness. The prophet discussed large principles, true for all time—principles social, political, ecclesiastical, and principles of life, chiefly by largeness of heart, and sympathy of spirit with God's Spirit. *That is my conception of inspiration.*

"The inspiration of the Bible is a large subject. I hold it to be inspired, not dictated. It is the word of God—the word of man; as the former, perfect; as the latter, imperfect. God the Spirit, as the Sanctifier, does not produce absolute perfection of human character; God the Spirit, as an Inspirer, does not produce absolute perfection of human knowledge; and for the same reason in both cases,—the human element which is mixed up—else there could have been no progressive dispensations.

"I hold it, therefore, as a proof of the inspiration of the Bible, and divinely wise, to have given a spiritual revelation, i. e., a revelation concerning the truths of the soul and its relation to God, in popular and incorrect language. Do not mistake that word *incorrect;* incorrect is one thing, false another."

8. *Hare.*

Archdeacon J. C. Hare († 1855), in common with other representatives of the Broad-church school, attributes inspiration to the common grace of God's quickening and enlightening Spirit, shared by the sacred writers in common with other Christians, but possessed in greater measure. His general view is expressed in a quotation which he makes approvingly from Ackermann, a German theologian.

"Theologians have not infrequently been guilty of a gross error with regard to the biblical idea of inspiration, from looking upon it as mechanical instead of dogmatical. * * * Hence they ought never to have adopted or encouraged the crude notion that persons under inspiration were like so many drawers, wherein the Holy Ghost put such and such things, which they then took out as something ready-made, and laid before the world, so that their recipiency with reference to the Spirit inspiring them was like that of a letter box. Whereas, inspiration, according to the Bible, is to be regarded as a vivifying and animating operation on the spiritual faculty in man, by which its energy and capacity are extraordinarily heightened, so that his powers of internal perception discern things spread out before them clearly and distinctly, which at other times lay beyond his range of vision, and were dark and hidden."[1]

9. *Maurice.*

The views of Maurice († 1872) on the question of inspiration were determined partly by his own subjective tendency and mystical turn of mind, and partly by his unbounded admiration for Coleridge, and the readiness with which he yielded to the formative influence of that profound thinker.

The nature of the operation of the Holy Spirit upon the minds of the sacred writers was, in his opinion, essentially the same in character with that enjoyed by Christian believers of the present day. Thus he says explicitly: "We must forego the demand which we make on the conscience of young men, when we compel them to declare that they regard the inspiration of the Bible as generically unlike that which God bestows on his children in this day."[2] He also denounces the common and orthodox course of setting up the Bible as a book which incloses all that may lawfully be called inspiration, and predicts that it will lead to a general alienation from the sacred records, and a wide-spread unbelief in Christianity.[3]

10. *Stanley.*

The late Dean of Westminster († 1881) has usually been regarded as a typical representative of the Broad-church school of English theology. His later writings, however, would seem to indicate somewhat *extreme* negative opinions. The first difficulty is, that his positions are implied rather than explicitly stated in his writings. One may feel a reasonable confidence of understanding him, and yet hesitate to attempt the formulation of his theory. For a long time his views in biblical criticism were tacitly associated with those of Colenso; his more recent attitude, however, has been identified with that of Mr. Robertson Smith, though high official station in the church may have dictated caution in avowing it. Some of his warmest admirers have lately

---

[1] *Mission of the Comforter,* 1 : 500.
[2] *Theological Essays,* McMillan, 1853, p. 339.
[3] Id., 349.

declared it impossible to tell from his published writings, whether he had any faith in the supernatural or not. One has bluntly asserted that 'he did not credit the miraculous history of Jesus Christ himself.'

11. *Jowett.*

Mr. Benjamin Jowett sets forth his views on the question of inspiration in the appendix of his Commentary on the Epistle to the Romans. Unfortunately for the writer, this book is not now at hand. An approximate idea of his position, however, may be gathered from his miscellaneous theological essays, which are easily accessible. In one,[1] after enumerating various opinions entertained, he says: "There is no foundation for any of the higher or supernatural views of inspiration in the gospels or epistles. Apostolic writings nowhere lead us to suppose that their authors were free from errors or infirmity."

It is quite in keeping with this utterance, that he should see imperfect or opposite aspects in different books of the Old Testament, variations of fact in the gospels, and inaccuracies of thought and language in the writings of Paul.

We now come to a group of writers, of orthodox instincts, and generally reputed soundness on this especial question, who have, however, this more particularly in common, that they admit different *degrees* of inspiration in the sacred records. In so doing, they follow the example of Lowth, Whitby, Doddridge and others.

12. *J. Pye Smith.*

Dr. Smith († 1851) speaks first for a careful distinction of revelation from inspiration. The former he makes to be the 'communication of knowledge not otherwise attainable, by immediate divine influence on the human mind.' The latter consists in 'qualifying the recipient of revelation to communicate the revealed knowledge to his fellow-creatures with perfect certainty and accuracy.'[2]

Inspiration may exist without revelation, as when one by divine appointment faithfully transmits to others information previously

---

[1] Essay on *Interpretation of Scripture. Essays and Reviews,* 380.
[2] *Scrip. Testim. to Messiah,* 1: 24.

gained through any of the providentially appointed means of acquiring it.¹

Among the author's conclusions regarding Holy Scripture are:

a. That evidence does not warrant the belief that all parts of the Old Testament were immediately dictated by the Holy Spirit, and possess the same kind of inspiration.²

b. Different subjects require different kinds or degrees of inspiration. A historian, relating what he learned from various trustworthy sources, would need divine influences of a different nature from those required to enable one to penetrate into future ages, or declare the hitherto secret counsels of the Deity. There must be revelation in the one case, while in the other it was sufficient if the writer was directed to the proper use of materials, and was preserved from mistake and misrepresentation.³

c. It was consistent with complete inspiration that the writers should be left to the free exercise of their own mental powers in the use of words, phrases and manner. Individual peculiarities would be preserved, but the matter would be of divine and infallible truth.⁴

Dr. Smith held, however, that when occasion required the divine suggestion of words or clauses, then miraculous intervention took place.⁵

13. *Wilson.*

Daniel Wilson, bishop of Calcutta († 1858), conceded both divine and human agency in the formation of the Scriptures,—the plenary influence of the Almighty Spirit, and yet the free exercise of the characteristic faculties of the writers.⁶

He sums up his idea of the *nature* of inspiration as follows: "We attribute such an inspiration to the minds of the sacred writers as exempted them from all error whatever in the communication of the divine will, and gave to every part of their declarations its full sanction as the infallible word of God; and at

---

¹ *Script. Test. &c.*, I: 24.
² Id., 27.
³ Id., 61.
⁴ Id. ib.
⁵ Id., 59.
⁶ *Evidences of Christianity*, Vol. I, Lect. XIII, p. 319.

the same time, allowed to each writer the free exercise of all his natural powers, and the delivery of the divine revelation according to his own habits and associations."[1]

As to the *extent* of inspiration, he distinguished four degrees or kinds.

a. That of *suggestion*—including such communications of the Holy Spirit as suggested and dictated minutely every part of the truths delivered.

b. That of *direction*—or such assistance as left the writers to describe the matter revealed in their own way, directing only the mind in the exercise of its powers.

c. That of *elevation*—adding a greater strength and vigor to the efforts of the mind than the writers could otherwise have attained.

d. That of *superintendency*—or the watchful care which preserved generally from anything being put down, derogatory to the revelation with which it was connected.[2]

This lowest kind, being always operative in the minds of the sacred writers, is carefully defined as to its sphere. Bishop Wilson concludes that it reached even to the least circumstances and most casual allusions of the sacred writers, in the proportion which each bore to the revelation itself.[3]

14. *Henderson.*

The well known work of Dr. Henderson needs little further reference than the notice of his five-fold distinction of degrees in inspiration, viz.: those of *divine excitement, invigoration, superintendence, guidance,* and *direct revelation.*

He held that the part taken by the Holy Spirit was confined to that which was necessary to make a divinely authoritative record; all the rest was left to men, e. g. the use of historical material and the choice of words.

Though objecting thus to verbal inspiration, Dr. Henderson says there is no material difference between himself and advocates of the opposite view, as he holds the sacred writers to have been 'always secured by celestial influence against the adoption of any

---

[1] *Evidences of Christianity,* Vol. I, Lect. XIII: 321.
[2] Id., 323.
[3] Id., 325.

forms of speech or collocations of words that would have injured the exhibition of divine truth, or that did not adequately give it expression."

15. *Browne.*

Among the latest works written from this point of view, is that of Walter R. Browne on 'The Inspiration of the New Testament.'[2]

This author distinguishes three distinct states of inspiration in the writers of Scripture, as follows:

a. "*Direct Inspiration*, when the writer is merely transcribing a revelation from God, made immediately to himself; and even in the transcription has a supernatural power working in and controlling him.

b. *Indirect Inspiration*, when the same controlling power operates, but when the matter recorded, although supernatural, is known to the writer, mainly at least, by the ordinary channels of information. This matter may be either supernatural words (as in the case of Christ's discourses given in the gospels), or else merely supernatural deeds, or arrangements; and the extent and nature of the controlling power will be different in these different cases.

To distinguish classes (a) and (b), we may say briefly that the writer is in the first a *messenger*, in the second, a *historian*.

c. *Preventive Inspiration*, when the matters are wholly within the writer's knowledge, and at the same time of no immediate supernatural import, being in general a mere filling in of details. Here the writer will simply be left to himself, to tell his story in his own way; and the only work of inspiration will be to *prevent* the introduction of any serious error, such as could not be detected by the readers of later generations, and might produce evil results."[3]

Compare also on Degrees in Inspiration.
Hill, *Lectures on Divinity*, p. 156.
Dick, *Essay on Inspiration*, p. 8; *also Lects. on Theol.*, I: 115.

Some general similarity of view, at least upon the question engaging our attention, may be detected in the writings of the several divines now to be mentioned.

---

[1] *Divine Inspiration.*
[2] C. Keegan Paul & Co., London, 1880.
[3] *Inspiration of the New Testament*, pp. 144–5.

16. *Conybeare.*

W. D. Conybeare († 1857), held with reference to—

a. The *nature* of inspiration—that the influence of the divine Spirit so guided and guarded the sacred writers as to suggest all essential and appropriate truth, and to preserve from all error. He rejected the notion of *degrees* in inspiration, as unnecessary, and unsupported by facts.

b. The *extent* of inspiration—that the divine influence extended not to verbal expression, but only to the securing of a certain and infallible standard of religious truth, from which there could be no appeal. In points not concerning this, guidance was not needed nor imparted. Conybeare, for example, doubts if inspiration extended to all of Paul's allusions to Jewish chronology. He strenuously insists, however, that in matters bearing in any way upon religion, no such allowances can be made.[1]

17. *Alford.*

The late Dean Alford († 1871) entertained very decided opinions upon the question of inspiration, which he sets forth in the Introduction to his Greek Testament, and incidentally brings out with great clearness in the body of the Commentary.

He says that inspiration did not make of the sacred writers mere channels for the transmission of infallible truth. The working of the Holy Spirit in them was analogous to his influence on every believer in Christ, viz., in the retention of individual character, thought and feeling, and in the gradual development of the ways and purposes of God in their minds. As their situation and office was peculiar and unexampled, so for its fulfillment peculiar and unexampled gifts were bestowed upon them. One of these, in the case of the apostles, was the recalling to their minds by the Holy Spirit of those things which our Lord had said.[2]

Our author contends that divine superintendence, as exercised in the composition of the gospels, extended no farther than that general leading, which, in main and essential points, ensured harmony between the writers. He is strong in the conviction that the phenomena of the gospels are inconsistent with the strict

---

[1] *Lects. on Theology,* London, 1836.
[2] *Proleg. Greek Test.,* Ch. I, § VI: 8.

verbal theory. He admits actual discrepancies in the evangelic narrative, and yet declares for 'plenary inspiration,' properly understood and defined.¹

His precise view of the *nature* of inspiration is contained in the following utterance: "The inspiration of the sacred writers, I believe to have consisted in the fulness of the influence of the Holy Spirit, specially raising them to, and enabling them for, their work,—*in a manner which distinguishes them from all other writers in the world, and their work from all other works.*"²

18. *Browne.*

Bishop Harold Browne contributed an essay on inspiration to the volume entitled "Aids to Faith," written in reply to "Essays and Reviews."

He holds that definite theories of inspiration are doubtful and dangerous, for the reason that while there are clearly both divine and human elements in the complex product going by this name, it is difficult to define the exact relation of the two.³

The *human* side of the Bible comes out in the different styles of the writers, and in apparent slight discrepancies in stating matters of detail. The few unimportant divergences which occur are of great apologetic value, as proving among other things the independence of the writers.⁴

The *divine* side of the Scriptures, or the genuine supernatural element, appears in infallible foreknowledge and actual predictions of future events, i. e. in *prophecy*.⁵

This undeniable fact differentiates biblical inspiration from that of mere genius. It cannot be explained on the principle of the simple exaltation of intuitional consciousness" (see Morell below), but proves an actual communication of the divine will to mankind, through the prophetic and other books of the Old Testament as channels.

What holds good of the Old Testament, holds good also *a fortiori* of the New; for no one could contend that the apostles—

---
¹ *Prolog. Gk. Test.*, Ch. I, § VI: 21.
² Id., ib.
³ *Aids to Faith*, 349.
⁴ Id., 356.
⁵ Id., 357.
⁶ Id., 359.

'with Christ's own mission, with the gift of tongues and miraculous powers, with the special promises of the Comforter and guidance by him into all truth, and with the assurance of Christ's own presence—were in a worse position, or more liable to error than the prophets.'[1]

The essential thing is infallibility in things pertaining to God and religious truth. Yet with all the pains and ingenuity which have been bestowed upon the subject, no charge of error, even in matters of human knowledge, has ever yet been substantiated against any of the writers of the Scriptures.[2] If the case had been otherwise, there would still be no cause for disquietude, so long as the supernatural element was such, both in character and extent, as to secure infallible truth in things divine.

19. *Farrar.*

We may note here the definition of inspiration given by the learned A. S. Farrar, in his 'Critical History of Free Thought:'[3]

"Inspiration is, if analyzed psychologically, probably a form of the 'reason;' but, if viewed theologically, it is an elevated state of this faculty, brought about by the miraculous and direct operation of God's Spirit: so that in this view it differs in kind, and not merely in depth from human genius."[4]

A series of writers holding more radical opinions now demand our notice.

20. *Davidson.*

Dr. S. Davidson asserts that inspiration did not lift man above error. It did not confer upon the sacred writers the attribute of infallibility. They were still peccable men, but, possessing the Spirit of God in remarkable degree, were gifted with peculiar insight into his mind.

Their own subjectivity mingled with and formed part of their inspiration. We take them as guides to faith and practice generally, without adopting all that they propounded, or believing that they could foretell future events.[5]

---

[1] *Aids to Faith*, 359.
[2] Id., 367.
[3] *Bampton Lects.*, 1862.
[4] Id. pp. 40, 470.
[5] *Introd. to New Testament*, 1: 14–15.

21. *Warrington.*

Geo. Warrington quotes with approval in his treatise,[1] Arnold's statement that 'the faculties of an inspired man are left in their natural state, except so far as regards the especial message with which he is charged.'

Summing up the results of his investigations of Scripture facts and phenomena, he declares,

a. Inspiration does not extend to the letter, but is confined to the spirit of the Bible.

b. The divine influence does not extend to statements regarded as narratives of matters of fact, but is confined to spiritual teaching, the question of personal sentiments being left undecided.

c. There is no reason to regard any portion of this teaching as uninspired, even when colored by personal or historical influences; there is rather every reason to regard the *whole* as inspired.

22. *Robertson Smith.*

To most conservative scholars it can scarcely seem less than absurd to speak of a theory of inspiration as held by Professor Robertson Smith. Yet he professes to have such a theory, and that the only correct one. He declares it consistent with the Westminster standards, and variant only from their traditional interpretation. It is rather incidentally developed than explicitly stated in his answer to the libel brought against him in due course of ecclesiastical procedure, and in his volume, 'The Old Testament in the Jewish Church.' It can really be deduced only from a summary of the results of his destructive work upon the Jewish canon. The design and limits of this article forbid the attempt to present such a résumé.

A few apparently clear conclusions, however, may be deduced. He professes to find both a divine and a human element in the Bible. The *latter*, the larger of the two, furnishes a fair field for the application of the principles of historical criticism. It is not only right, but imperatively necessary, that all parts of the Scriptures wherein this element is controlling, be subjected to precisely the same critical tests and treatment as are applied to literary works in general. Opinions will necessarily vary as to how much can remain of a particular passage or book after Mr. Smith has

---

[1] *Inspiration of the Scriptures—Its Limits and its Effects.*

actually proceeded to exercise upon it the critical office. Infallibility certainly finds no province *here*.

The *divine* element in the Scriptures is left indefinite as to the scope of its application. Apparently no more is conceded than that it concerns such a 'knowledge of God and of his will as is necessary to salvation.' The author would probably make it inclusive simply of 'God's commands, threatenings and promises addressed to our faith, and above all, of the gospel offer of Christ to us.' The ground of faith in the divine origin and character of the truths contained within the Scriptures is not to be found in any external testimonies to an objective revelation, but simply and solely in the subjective convictions of personal experience wrought within the heart by the power of the Holy Ghost. This being accepted, it is hard to see what functions yet remain to supernatural inspiration.

Better, however, than any attempted analysis of the views of Prof. Smith, may be a few citations from his latest published works. Thus he says:

"The persuasion that in the Bible God himself speaks words of love and life to the soul, is the essence of the Christian's conviction as to the truth and authority of the Scriptures.[1]

"Of this I am sure at the outset, that the Bible does speak to the heart of man in words that can come only from God—that no historical research can deprive me of this conviction, or make less precious the divine utterances that speak straight to the heart.

"For the language of those words is so clear that no re-adjustment of their historical setting can conceivably change the substance of them.

"The supreme truths which speak to every believing heart, the way of salvation, which is the same in all ages, the clear voice of God's love, so tender and personal and simple that a child can understand it—these are things which must abide with us, and prove themselves mighty from age to age, apart from all scientific study.[2]

"The inspired writers were so led by the Spirit that they perfectly understood and perfectly recorded every word which God spoke to their hearts.[3]

---

[1] *Old Testament*, etc., p. 4.

[2] Id., p. 28.

[3] Id., p. 9.

"The Bible is a book of experimental religion, in which the converse of God with his people is depicted in all its stages, up to the full and abiding manifestation of saving love in the person of Jesus Christ. God has no message of love to the believing soul, which the Bible does not set forth."[1]

These utterances, in their detached form, have a certain sound and savor of orthodoxy; but it remains true, nevertheless, that the views of Prof. Smith, as actually applied to the canon, are subversive of all belief in inspiration, at least in the sense commonly understood and accepted by the orthodox consciousness of the church.

The next group of writers is, if possible, still more strongly pronounced in its expression of negative views.

23. *Morell.*

Morell, a disciple of Schleiermacher, and essentially at one with the *advanced* Broad-church school in views upon our subject, distinguishes revelation and inspiration, but regards them as two different sides of one divine act. The former is an exercise of power by which God presents the realities of the spiritual world immediately to the human mind; the latter is that especial influence wrought in the mind of the subject, by which he is enabled to grasp those realities in perfect fulness and integrity. God made a revelation of himself to the world in Jesus Christ, but it was the inspiration of the apostles which enabled them clearly to discern it.[2] The result of the two is to produce in the human mind a state of intuition, whose phenomena are so extraordinary, that we at once separate them from any of the ordinary principles of human development. Yet this agency is applied in perfect consistency with the laws and natural operations of our spiritual nature.

Inspiration does not imply anything generically new in the actual processes of the human mind; it does not involve any form of intelligence essentially different from what we already possess; it indicates rather the elevation of the religious consciousness, and with it, of course, the power of spiritual vision to a degree of intensity peculiar to the individual thus highly favored by God.[3]

---

[1] *Old Testament*, pp. 13–14.
[2] *Philosophy of Religion*, 148; Appleton's Edition.
[3] Id., 148.

Having denied to the sacred writers miraculous powers, verbal dictation or any distinct commission to their work from God,[1] he proceeds to affirm the generic resemblance of biblical inspiration to that of genius. Genius consists in the possession of a remarkable power of intuition with reference to some particular object, a power which arises from the inward nature of a man being brought into unusual harmony with that object in its reality and its operations.[2]

The *difference* of the two kinds of inspiration lies simply in the nature of the objects apprehended, and in the exciting cause of the inward mental elevation to which that apprehension is due.[3]

24. *MacNaught.*

This author carries out the naturalistic theory to its farthest limits. He defines inspiration to be 'that action of the divine Spirit by which, apart from any idea of infallibility, all that is good in man, beast or matter is originated and sustained.'[4] There is to him no distinction whatever between inspiration and genius. He makes no question that David, Solomon, Isaiah, or Paul would have spoken of everything which may with propriety be called a work of genius, or of cleverness, or of holiness, as works of the Spirit of God, written by divine inspiration.[5]

Every thing good in any person or thing is inspired, and the value of any book claiming the quality of inspiration depends upon the amount actually exhibited, and the importance of the truths it teaches. Milton, Shakspeare, Bacon, Canticles, the Apocalypse, the Sermon on the Mount, and the eighth chapter of Romans are all inspired; but which of them is the most valuable, and therefore most truly inspired, is to be determined by consideration of its character, tendency, and beneficial effects as seen in its history.[6] As above indicated, Mr. MacNaught discovers inspiration in rational and irrational creatures, in matter organic and inorganic. He finds it in the instinct of the owl, hears it in

---

[1] *Philos. of Relig.*, 159.
[2] Id. 173.
[3] Hodge, *Syst. Theol.*, I: 176.
[4] *Doctrine of Inspiration*, 196.
[5] Id. 192.
[6] Id. ib

the rushing of the wind, and sees it in the springing of the blade of grass.

He is able also to argue, to his own mind conclusively, from the lack of infallibility in these acts and phenomena of nature, to a similar want of infallibility in the writings of inspired men.

25. *Newman.*

No further statement will be needful as to Mr. F. W. Newman's views concerning inspiration than to refer to his volume, 'Phases of Faith,' especially chaps. IV. ff. This gentleman has made the discovery that 'a book revelation is a contradiction in terms', that an 'authoritative external revelation of moral and spiritual truth is essentially impossible to man; and that what God reveals to us, he reveals within, through the medium of our moral and spiritual senses.'[1]

It would certainly be a sudden and violent transition, were we to pass from the extreme rationalism of such writers as have last engaged our attention, to a detailed consideration of the reactionary orthodoxy of writers like Haldane, Bannerman and others. We shall content ourselves with a simple reference to their treatises:

Haldane—"*Verbal Inspiration of the Scriptures.*"
Bannerman—"*Inspiration of the Holy Scriptures.*"
Elliott—"*Inspiration of the Holy Scriptures*" (more moderate).
Given—"*Revelation, Inspiration, and the Canon.*"

VII. Greek and Roman Catholic Churches.

Our historical sketch may properly conclude with a reference to the doctrine of inspiration as held by the modern Greek and Roman Catholic churches. For the views of various Protestant bodies on the subject, it will be sufficient to refer to the denominational literatures, in general, easily accessible.

1. *The Greek Church.*

Questions as to the nature and extent of inspiration are hardly known as subjects of discussion here. All are content with the

---

[1] *The Soul,* p. 59.

statement that the Holy Spirit is the author and communicator of Scripture, and that the prophets and apostles are the media through which that communication is made to men.[1]

2. *The Roman Catholic Church.*

The Catholic doctrine of inspiration has been recently set forth by Archbishop Gibbons,[2] and his statements may be accepted as sufficiently authoritative.

The Vatican Council declared: "The books of the Old and New Testaments are to be received as sacred and canonical, * * * because, having been written by inspiration of God, they have God for their author, and have been handed down to the Church herself as such."

Catholic theologians in answer to the question 'What is inspiration?'[3] would define it as 'a supernatural help whereby God, at various times down to the end of the apostolic age, enlightened the minds of certain men that they might know the truths which he wished to deliver in writing to his church, and moved their will to write them and nothing else.'

As the Bible is not written to teach science, the sacred writers use the language of their time. We must not look in the Bible for what passes for scientific accuracy in the nineteenth century. Still Catholics hold that, rightly interpreted, the Bible is not only infallible in what concerns faith and morals, but that, moreover, it contains no historical misstatement or error about physical facts.[4]

K. GENERAL CONCLUSIONS FROM THE WHOLE SURVEY.

If now we ask what general conclusions may be safely and legitimately drawn from that *limited province* of the historical doctrine of inspiration which we have surveyed, it may be replied:

1. Inspiration, in the sense of a communication of the divine will to men through chosen messengers, has been matter of

---

[1] *Bib. Sac.*, Oct., 1864, p. 821.
[2] *North American Review*, 1878, pp. 324 ff.
[3] Id., p. 326.
[4] Id., p. 327.

general belief among heathen and Christians, Jews and Gentiles, in every age. It readily responds to the triple test of Catholicity, viz., acceptance "semper, ubique, ab omnibus."

II. *Theories* as to the nature and extent of biblical inspiration should be always, and in great measure have actually been, broadly distinguished from the *fact* itself. Unanimity with reference to the latter is the more abundantly proved by the comparative absence of dogmatic speculations upon the former, during the first fifteen centuries of the history of the church.

III. Abandoning the common, but really useless attempt at a rigid classification of the various theories of inspiration, we may yet say with confidence that no single one has ever commanded sufficiently general assent to entitle it to rank (as party zealots would have it) as 'the immemorial doctrine of the church of God.'

IV. History furnishes conclusive evidence that no doctrine of inspiration can hope for general acceptance in the church, which fails to accord full recognition to the co-existence, co-activity and harmonious relation of the two factors—divine and human—in the same.

All efforts wholly to displace, or unduly to exalt the one or the other, will be met by a more or less prompt, and certainly a strong reaction against the sole supremacy of this, and a like re-assertion of the factor which is denied or undervalued. The doctrine in its historical development has given evidence of a kind of self-corrective power, which, in the long run at least, is sure to make its presence and efficient operation manifest.

V. If the truth of the foregoing statement be conceded, it is plain that the doctrine of inspiration, properly so called, can have nothing to fear from the attacks of modern biblical criticism, be they those of avowed rationalism, of pseudo-evangelicalism (whose loud professions of allegiance to confessional standards scarcely suffice to conceal its really *negative* spirit and intent), or of reactionary orthodoxy and bigotry.

The trend of opinion at the present day is, as seen above, toward a fuller recognition of the human element in the Scriptures; and bold assertions are made of errors manifold in fact, and even in doctrine (which in a historic revelation like the Bible arises out of fact), but it is to be remembered on the other hand:

1. That scepticism in every age, thus far, has found, as concern-

ing attacks upon the Scriptures, that assertion was one thing, but proof and carrying of general conviction quite another.

2. That its assaults have uniformly resulted in establishing the truth denied, upon a more solid basis than before, and, by clearing it from misapprehension and ambiguity, in securing for it more complete and symmetrical development than would otherwise have been possible.

If the outcome of present controversies should prove different, it would indeed be 'a new thing under the sun.'

It is matter of fact that to-day, as the result of the very criticism which is viewed in so many quarters with alarm, and pending the solution of many difficult and disputed questions, the general fabric of the Scriptures, 'apart from the question of its inspiration, stands on a firmer footing than it did a century ago.' This, by the unwilling confession of rationalism itself.

Surely then, simple-hearted faith in the divine oracles may well rest quietly, thank God for that 'whereto it has already attained,' and take courage for the future.

MISCELLANEOUS WORKS ON THE SUBJECT OF INSPIRATION:

Curtis, *Human Element in the Inspiration of the Scriptures.* Appletons, 1867.
Lewis, *Divine-Human in the Scriptures.* Carter & Bros., 1860.
Jamieson, *Inspiration of the Holy Scriptures.* Edinburgh, W. Blackwood & Sons, 1873.
Lord, *Inspiration not Guidance or Intuition.* Randolph, 1858.
Wordsworth, *Inspiration of Holy Scriptures.* London, Rivingtons, 1851.
Lee, *Inspiration of the Scriptures—Nature and Proof.* Carters, 1857.

See also:

Westcott, *Introduction to the Study of the Gospel,* pp. 1–42. MacMillan.
Hodge, *Systematic Theology, I:* 151–82.

INDEX OF AUTHORS.

	PAGE.		PAGE.
Abelard,	31	Erasmus,	37
Agobard,	30	Eusebius of Cæsarea,	23, 25
Alford,	98	Euthymius Zigabenus,	30
Anselm,	31	Farrar, A. S.,	100
Aquinas, Thomas,	31	Fox, G.,	56
Arndt,	56	Fridegisus,	30
Arnold, Thomas,	90		
Athanagoras,	18	Gaussen,	86
Augustine,	26, 27	Gerhard,	46, 48
		Gibbons, Archbp.,	106
Baier,	47	Godet,	87
Barclay,	56	Gregory (the Great),	26
Basil (the Great),	27	Griesbach,	64
Baxter,	59	Grotius,	53
Bellarmine,	51		
Browne, Bp. Harold,	99	Hare, J. C.,	92
Browne, W. R.,	97	Heber,	89
Bugenhagen,	42	Henderson,	96
Bullinger,	42	Hengstenberg,	84
Burnet, G.,	58	Henke,	65
Buxtorffs,	50	Herder,	65
		Hofmann,	82
Calamy,	69	Hoburg,	56
Calixtus,	50	Hollaz,	47, 48, 49
Calovius,	48, 49	Irenæus,	14, 15, 22
Calvin,	41		
Cassiodorus,	26	Jerome,	27
Chrysostom,	26	John of Damascus,	29
Clarke, S.,	69	Josephus,	10
Clement of Alex.	15, 16, 20, 23	Jowett,	94
Coleridge,	90	Junilius,	28
Conybeare, W. D.,	98	Justin Martyr,	14, 15, 18, 19, 22
Cyprian,	16	Le Clerc,	54
Cyril of Jerusalem,	15	Limborch,	53
Davidson, S.,	100	Luther,	38
DeWette,	74	Mac Naught,	104
Doddridge,	70	Maimonides,	35, 36
Düsterdieck,	83	Martensen,	80
Elwert,	77	Maurice,	93
Episcopius,	54	Melancthon,	40

INDEX OF AUTHORS.

	PAGE.
Meylan,	87
Michaelis,	64
Middleton,	72
Miltiades,	20
Mohammed,	4
Morell,	103
Musaeus,	50
Neander,	78
Novatian,	22
Origen,	15, 16, 20, 21, 23
Owen,	59
Paley,	88
Parry,	89
Pfaff,	62
Phillippi,	79
Philo,	11, 18, 19
Pictet,	51
Pighius,	52
Piscator,	51
Plato,	6
Plutarch,	7
Priestly,	89
Quenstedt,	46, 47, 48, 49
Robertson,	91
Rothe,	80
Sakya-Mouni (Buddha),	3
Savonarola,	34
Schleiermacher,	74
Semler,	61, 63
Simon, R.,	52

	PAGE.
Smith, J. Pye,	94
Smith, W. Robertson,	101
Socinus, F.,	55
Spencer,	57
Spinoza,	55, 61
Stapfer,	66
Stanley,	93
Stier,	79
Swedenborg,	66
Tauler,	33
Tertullian,	14, 16, 17, 19, 22, 23
Theodore of Mopsuestia,	27, 28
Theodoret,	26, 27
Theophilus,	14, 15, 18
Tholuck,	82
Thomas Aquinas,	31
Tillotson,	57
Töllner,	62
Twesten,	76
Van Oosterzee,	84
Wakefield,	73
Warburton,	71
Wegscheider,	73
Weigel,	56
Wessel,	35
Whitby,	68
Wiclif,	34
Wilson, Bp. Daniel,	95
Zoroaster,	3
Zwingle,	40

www.ingramcontent.com/pod-product-compliance
Lightning Source LLC
Chambersburg PA
CBHW030405170426
43202CB00010B/1496